A WRITER'S
GUIDE TO
CREATIVE
BREAKTHROUGH

BURN
Wild

Christi Krug

Keep stoking that fire... You truly

BURN Wild, and will keep on burning wild!

~ Christi

SQUIGGLE PRESS

ISBN: 978-0-615-64118-8

All the song lyrics used are in the public domain.

Portions of "Authenticity," in different form, have been published in *Personal Journaling Magazine,* February 2003.

Portions of the "The Incineration of Procrastination," in different form, have been published in *Writer's Guide to Creativity,* August 2003.

"Creating through a Crisis," in different form, was published in *Writer's Digest,* March 2004.

The following authors have graciously granted permission to use these works:

"Barn," by Sage Cohen, *Like the Heart, the World,* Queen of Wands Press, 2007.
Poem excerpt by Kate Gray, from "What Poets Do," *Another Sunset We Survive,* Cedar House Books, 2007.
"boy's first pencil," by Harold Johnson, *Dixon Ticonderoga,* Redcat Press, 2010.
Poem excerpt by Toni Partington, from "Sustained on Leftovers," *Wind Wing,* Toni Partington, 2010.
"Ink," by Paulann Petersen, *Kindle,* Mountains and Rivers Press, 2008.

Printed in the United States of America

Squiggle Press

Dedication

For my husband, Paul Krug,
who makes so many dreams possible.

Table of Contents

INK

Night in a bottle,
stars swimming
inside glass.

When we quit
dipping our pens,
when we emptied

darkness out of
its vessel,
did we stop

a constellation
from writing itself
onto a page?

by Paulann Petersen

Introduction

Remember when you wrote whole chapters in the sand
and flight was the nexus of wish and might

—from "Sustained on Leftovers," a poem by Toni Partington

DOES CREATING have a place in your life? As children, most of us had boundless fantasies about what we could make and do. As years passed, however, these dreams seemed a waste of time.

Perhaps you imagined being a poet or a glass artist, a woodworker or a novelist, a gourmet chef or a mime. You fancied yourself a rock star, fashion designer, songwriter or tap dancer.

As life went on, the demands of work and relationships cooled the embers of these dreams. You learned to keep them secret. Gradually, fear soaked your creativity, like a wave washing over driftwood.

This book will help you bring back the fire. It will teach you how to enjoy your creativity rather than spend your energy fighting, procrastinating, resisting or denying it.

This book is for people who were once children who staged homemade plays or made up jokes or decorated the wall with Mom's lipstick. Who invented recipes and composed love songs and flew passenger kites for caterpillars. Who built hideouts and mapped treasure hunts. Who wore superhero capes and made paper boats and changed clothes six times a day.

This book is for people who've always wanted to create with words or images, with poetry or play-dough. It could be you tried and gave up, because deep down you never felt like a writer or an artist. This book will help you rekindle that faith. This book is for people who long to let their imagination play a daily role in their lives.

This is a book about living and writing. It offers the courage to do both more creatively.

Why I Wrote this Book

When I was a kid, I loved to draw, make up stories, paint pictures, write poems and make messes. Parents and teachers said nice things about my creations (except the messes), and I loved this. I thought: *I can be a writer! I can be an artist!* My grandmother submitted one of my cartoons to the *Seattle Post Intelligencer* where it was printed. My mom photocopied my drawings, making a coloring book for kids at church. I borrowed an old typewriter and submitted poems which were published nationally—once, twice, three times. But a strange thing happened. Gradually, I came to value only the things that others valued.

As a young adult I would enter writing contests but I was distracted by opinions. Did other people think I was gifted? Could I get published? No longer was I creating for the joy.

When my writing got rejected, or when people didn't compliment my art, I decided I was mistaken about having talent. A person had to grow up and get a real job, after all. So I did that, and forgot about writing anything "real."

Instead, I tried my hand at journaling. The problem was, I couldn't keep anything in a journal. I would take an Exacto knife and slice away the single page I had managed to write with "mistakes" on it. I hated everything I wrote.

Then I met Noelle, who wrote in her journal every day. She would transform an empty notebook into a companion brimming with musings and poetry, doodles, prayers and complaints. "How do you do it?" I asked.

She shrugged. "Nobody's going to see it but me. It doesn't *have* to be good."

I talked to creative people I knew. I stumbled on books explaining the dichotomy of the creative process: *Writing on Both Sides of the Brain* by

Henriette Anne Klauser and *Drawing on the Right Side of the Brain* by Betty Edwards. I discovered principles that had little to do with technique and a lot to do with mindset.

Over the next three years, I put the principles into practice. I trained myself to stop being intimidated about journaling, writing, or auditioning for a play. I practiced my creative dreams instead of denying them. Paradoxically, because I didn't care so much anymore, I could risk rejection. I submitted and sold freelance articles and stories. I was bringing new words into the world, and feeling the joy.

I began to meet people who admired my work and would sigh about their own lost ambition. "If only I was good enough, I would . . ." They had reasons for not writing or painting, doing stand-up comedy, or dancing. They were stifled by obligations, people, and circumstances, but most of all, by the idea that they weren't "good enough."

I wanted to share what I'd learned. I created the class, Wildfire Writing.

Students showed up. The prompts got them laughing and crying. They picked up their pens. They wrote. They reversed directions, firing up lost dreams.

Wildfire Writing students not only became writers, but also painters, photographers, gardeners and craftspeople as well as columnists, novelists and picture-book authors. Students crossed life-changing thresholds: losing forty pounds or standing up to a controlling spouse. The new ideas helped them to *live* better.

How to Use this Book

Read the chapters in any order. Write in this book. You don't have to wait until you take a vacation, retire, win the lottery, or stumble on a block of free time: start now. Do a ten or fifteen minute "spark" and feel the difference it can make in your day, week, month, year. This is your creative life. Live it!

Disclaimer #1:

This book will tap emotion. That's a shady thing to do. In our society we are distrustful of anything that encourages us to be emotional.

Once I met a tall, dramatic woman who said she wanted to be a writer. "But I can write only one or two sentences at a time," she said. She kept shifting on her feet and tossing her auburn hair behind her shoulders. "My words are all bottled up. I need help. I'm thinking about taking one of your classes."

I began to describe my approach in Wildfire Writing, but before I could get the words out, she blurted, "I can't do a touchy-feely class. Is this a touchy-feely class?"

"Yes," I said. "If you put it that way. It will help you get in touch with what you need to say."

"Um, no thanks," she said, shaking her head, and fled the room. I understood. This was the very reason she couldn't put down more than a few words. She was terrified of her own feelings.

Disclaimer #2:

This is a feel-good book. It will support positive feelings and help you . . . well, *feel good*. It will make you feel good when you take in the concepts and act upon them. It can't make you feel good if you don't do anything about it. As Benjamin Disraeli said, "Action may not always bring happiness, but there is no happiness without action."

For those who dare, and aren't intimidated about making positive changes, you may gain insight into relationships. Or mountain climbing. Or prayer. You will come to understand your own creative process.

I didn't invent these principles. They have been recognized by artists and poets and writers throughout time. I have found some low-key ways that any busy person may put them into practice, fostering growth and awareness.

This is not a complicated manual asking for a sobering commitment. It's an invitation. *Oh, come and play, creative one.*

The invitation is for you.

CHAPTER ONE

Sparks

"Hark! The fire-alarm is sounding,
see, the air is lit with flames."

—from "Fire! Fire! Fire!" a song by T.B. Kelley

THERE'S A CREATIVE FIRE inside you ready to happen. You can't see or touch it, but sometimes you feel it. Even so, in the day to day, there are so many other things on your mind that the fire seems to fade. Besides, someone once told you that your poetry, or watercolor painting, or magic show wasn't all that brilliant.

A teacher's red pen may have slashed your pride. Or the question of money may have destroyed ambition. "That's fine for a hobby," Dad said about a poem, novel or cartoon, "but you can't make money at it." Whenever we glimpse our pens or paintbrushes or mosaic supplies, those words come back to us, and we find something else to do.

Fear drives us away from creativity. We're afraid of looking stupid, wasting time, whittling away our lives, making people angry, making people laugh, ending up at a curb with a cardboard sign. In short, we fear failure. But the prospect of success can also be terrifying. There's the unknown territory that means a loss of control, comfort and predictability.

Maybe you've bided your time with a matchbook of potential ideas, hidden away for later. Next chance, you were going to light that fire. Trouble is, the chance never happened. Your matches disappeared into a pocket somewhere and got lost.

You decided to get serious. But then you enrolled in a degree program or remodeled your kitchen or dated someone new or changed jobs or had a baby or moved cross-country. Last you checked, the fire was a fading wisp of smoke.

Without addressing our mental, emotional and spiritual states as creators, we will never sustain the creative fire.

We won't start projects or finish them. We'll putter. We'll raise an occasional puff of creativity, but it won't burn high and hot.

To light the wildfire, the first step is to honestly examine your creative life. Let's start by taking a look at writing.

Starting Mode

Uh-oh. Writing. Starting a writing project can be murder. At your desk in third period English, the blank paper stared you down with its watery blue lines and accusing white face. *Go ahead, dummy. You're a lousy speller.* (Tapping foot.) *Better come up with a dynamic opening.* (Chewing eraser.) *Watch that topic sentence!*

Wildfire Writing recognizes two opposing forces when it comes to creating. One mode is creative, one critical. They aren't necessarily "left brain" and "right brain" because the physiology is complex and research is ongoing. Regardless of any physical demarcation in the brain, you can feel the shift when you are working in one mode or the other.

Spiritual teachers call these two modes the flesh and the spirit, or the ego and the true self. Deep down, we all recognize what it means to act from the heart rather than the brain. The important thing is to recognize this distinction in your own life. I've named the two styles of thinking Dr. Codger and the Dream Kid, the seats of contrasting characteristics.

Dr. Codger	Dream Kid
Logic	Emotion
Structure	Free-flow
Analysis	Hunches
Order	Chance
Language	Storytelling
Labels	Essence
Editing	Creating
Plans	Spontaneity
Schedules	Timelessness
Revisions	Ideas
Work	Play

Dr. Codger is the mode in which we live our everyday lives—going to work, paying bills, fulfilling obligations. Always focused on results, Dr. Codger watches the clock, responsibly getting us where we need to go. Dream Kid, on the other hand, springs from fire. She is burning with curiosity and passionate about life. She savors experiences, whether or not they produce a particular result. Dream Kid dances with joy and sadness, intensity and exhilaration. Passionate, creative writing can only begin when this wild child strikes the first match.

In that conversation inside our heads during English class, Dr. Codger dominated. Dream Kid didn't get a word in edgewise. Unfortunately, many of us listened to Dr. Codger, thinking only he could provide the impetus for writing our essay. Truth is, Dream Kid is the lone supplier of ideas.

Most of the time our society trudges along seeking to appease the rules and regulations of Dr. Codger. Writing for fun seems purposeless—unless, of course, you can make a living at it.

So we send Dream Kid outside to play with the other children. Or, we envy her role in the lives of people lucky and talented enough to be dancers or novelists or children's book illustrators or musicians. With Dr. Codger as our guide, Dream Kid can't lead us to our own creating.

Check in with this Dream Kid of yours. Remember how it feels to let her take over.

Spark 1

Think back to an occasion when you completely lost track of yourself. You looked up from dancing or writing a letter or skiing down a mountain and realized that a huge chunk of time had elapsed.

• Close your eyes and relive the experience.

• What were you doing?

• What was Dream Kid saying?

• How did you feel?

Words people have used to describe their experiences: *thrilled, proud, surprised, natural, effortless, flowing.*

Jot down a word to describe this sensation. Now write another word or two. Whenever Dream Kid shows up, remember this feeling.

Spark 2

Call up a memory of yourself writing like a maniac. Did you ever produce a story, poem, Christmas letter, essay, or school newspaper article that made you proud? Imagine how you felt about this work and the ideas you were able to express. Complete the following sentences.

- *While I was writing, I felt . . .*
- *I enjoyed this project because . . .*
- *Positive feedback came in the form of . . .*

Soon you will feel this sense of accomplishment again.

Spark 3

Reflect on a time you felt completely alive, from your hair follicles to the soles of your feet. Think about what your body experienced.

- What did you see?
- What did you touch?
- What did you taste or smell?
- What did you hear?

Focus on the images and sensations, not the words. Then see if you can translate each sensation into a word or sentence. Forget trying to sound brilliant, just do the best you can. Notice how interesting it is to move from feeling to language.

CHAPTER TWO

Are You Licensed?

"I dare not break the seal! What fear, what doubt I feel."

—from "True Love from O'er the Sea," a song by H.B. Farnie

TWENTY-SOME YEARS AGO when I sold my first magazine article, I was raising a toddler and juggling priorities, babysitters, naptimes and chores. When I spent time writing I felt guilty about "neglecting my real duties." I wasn't convinced I had a right to do this.

So it is with our choices about time. We rush from on-ramp to exit ramp, churning minutes into miles and paychecks, chafing in checkout lines, lurching through parking lots. We toss kids off to school and catch them again like rebounding basketballs. We reel with bills to mail, teeth to fix, cars to service, lawns to mow, people to please, taxes to pay, meals to choke down, paperwork to stash, bodies to groom, cell phones to answer.

But who's in charge here, anyway?

More than any other force in your life, you must respect the fire of creativity. You must give yourself permission to spend time, money and effort—regardless of the outcome of your work. Only then can you negotiate the disappointments and needs of others around you. It all starts with a license.

So here it is. Sign it. Seal it. Display it for the authorities. Remind the world, every time they pass your refrigerator door that this is your right.

There are two versions of the license. The first is for writing, the second for everything else.

My License To Write

I, _____, am a writer.

This license grants me the right to write. I may do so whenever I choose. I can spend time, money and resources on developing my skills. I can try new forms and genres, with or without an outline. I can take on the task of any novel, poem, or scene, even when I don't know how to go about it. I have permission not to finish everything I start. I do not demand compensation, but welcome it when provided. As the owner of this writing license, I can write nonsense or dreck, making grammar, punctuation, and spelling errors. I can seek out fellow writers for support.

I do not require that the writing process be comfortable. I can persevere in completing projects I believe in. I will let writing be a force that helps to shape my life, guiding me into greater awareness of myself. I may decline obligations that inhibit my creativity or consume my time for writing.

I assert that I am the owner of unique feelings, perceptions, memories, opinions, ideas and observations. I will put forth my words. I will tell my stories.

Dated: _____

My Creative License

I, _____, am the owner of my own creativity. This license grants me the right to be creative whenever and wherever I choose, to try new forms of art, to dabble, experiment, invent, and make things up as I go along. I will not deny or relinquish my creative talents to any outside individual, group, or entity. I can make messes, devise plans, ask questions, take classes, and set aside time for creating. I will allow myself to grow. I can spend money on creative tools and seek out fellow creators with which to associate.

I may change my mind about any project at any time or set new goals as new desires unfold. I may rightfully decline obligations that inhibit my creativity or consume my time for creating.

I exercise my right to express my sensibilities in my own way. I am original and talented, with much to offer the world.

Dated: _____

CHAPTER THREE

Striking the Match

O for a Muse of fire, that would ascend
The brightest heaven of invention . . .

—Shakespeare, *Henry V*, Prologue

WHEN WAS THE LAST TIME you let yourself play? Play happens in Dream Kid mode, and it's the beginning of all creating. If you don't start with play, Dr. Codger will overpower your creativity with incessant demands and critical judgments.

Dream Kid is your accelerator, Dr. Codger your brake pedal. Operating both at once is as exasperating as driving with the brakes on. Engaging Dr. Codger while trying to create is the most common mistake in the creative process, especially writing. It can frustrate you to the point of giving up.

Mark Twain said, "Education consists mainly in what we have unlearned." Indeed, writing has historically been taught from Dr. Codger's perspective, and many of us need to overcome this training.

Remember that smooth sheet of scary white paper. Elbows on table and head in hands, our grades were at stake, our minds blank. This had to be perfect. Problem was, we couldn't think of a single thing to say.

Dr. Codger is obsessed with how well things are said. He's an intimidating taskmaster, but the truth is, he has no ideas. When we get into Dr. Codger mode, we can find any number of things wrong with our work. He is an astute critic and can tear anything apart in three seconds flat. But keep in mind his limitations. He can't produce a single thing on his own. He's like a movie critic who can point out flaws in a film, but when it comes to creating, cannot put together a simple flip book.

Enter Dream Kid. That is, if you're brave enough to give her permission to show up. Dream Kid gets her words tangled up, has messy handwriting, and isn't much of a speller. Yet she has a heart full of stories, observations and worthwhile things to say. When you read a story that chokes you up with tears or knocks you to the floor in gut-busting laughter, you know Dream Kid has been allowed to play.

Dream Kid is the creator. When we're listening to Dr. Codger rant about results and grades and correctness, we can't follow Dream Kid's lead. We can't create.

Think of a child learning to talk. When my daughter said her first sentence, she leaned forward in her high chair and pointed to a loaf of bread, her dark eyes snapping. "I want . . ." she said, and then pointed to a jar of blackberry jam, "dat . . . on *dat!*"

"You want jam on bread?" I said, rushing over.

She nodded.

"That's wonderful, honey!" *Dat on dat. Dat on dat!* I delighted in her genius all day. I wrote "Dat on dat," in her baby book. I called Dad at work: "Guess who said her first sentence!"

What parent would do otherwise? Imagine if I had shaken my head and put hands on hips. "Listen here, short stuff. What's this 'dat'? You need to enunciate clearly to get along in this world. And for heaven's sake, be specific!"

An affirming attitude is incredibly important with any art or craft, especially writing. Olympic trainers know that athletes perform at their peak when serene and relaxed, not tense with obsession over their goals. Always approach your creativity with the openness of the Dream Kid, not the ultimatums of Dr. Codger.

Elsewhere, we'll explore Dr. Codger's important role in refining a work. But remember: you can't light a match without Dream Kid. Shut up Dr. Codger for a while. Ignore, defy, displace, or distract him. Playtime is your starting line.

Spark 1

Go to a seashore, lakeshore, or park, and sit in the sand or dirt. Bring any of the following: a bucket, shovel, toy truck, pad or blanket, box of animal cookies. Ready? Now. One, two, three . . . play.

Spark 2

Buy stickers, whether happy faces or congratulating dinosaurs or stars for schoolwork. When you're tempted to criticize, give yourself a sticker instead. Plaster stickers on and around your writing or art.

CHAPTER FOUR

Passionate Discipline

"Now some are fond of studying,
and some are fond of sport."

—from a song by Geo. H. Macdermot

ONE OF MY CHILDREN'S writing mentors, Robin Jones Gunn, author of 82 books including the award-winning Christy Miller series, told me years ago about a conversation she frequently had. As a busy writer and mother of two young children, she'd get approached by admirers who said, "I just can't believe how disciplined you are!" Robin would graciously respond, "I'm not disciplined at all. I just love to write. Like most people, I always find time for what I love to do."

A creator must commit large amounts of time. But the secret to discipline, as Robin explained, is loving your work.

The problem with most creators is that we get caught up in results, outcomes, what-ifs and the possibility of failure. Then we lose the joy of our creative process. We don't focus on the part we love; instead we focus on what we fear and dread. Consequently, we lose the passion, and *then* have to drag ourselves to the grindstone.

A reverse way to capture passion is to cultivate the discipline first. In other words, don't wait for the muse before you paint, write, dance—do the thing that deep down you know you were meant to do. Study your calendar and set up a schedule for your work. Make this schedule a program that you stick to, no matter how uninspired you feel. Renowned choreographer Twyla Tharp in her book *The Creative Habit* points out that sticking to your program is "as much a part of the creative process as the lightning bolt of inspiration, maybe more."

Once you have a regular, disciplined schedule, you will have an abundance of opportunities to experience the joy of creating, and this will attract you magnetically, day after day. You'll hone your talents, producing far beyond your expectations. It will barely seem that you are working according to discipline, and when folks ask, you'll say: "Gosh, I just do this because

I love it!"

Spark

Choose a time for your daily creative work, setting aside everything else for ten to sixty minutes. Put everything you can into making this time inviting, comfortable and fun. Brew an exotic roast of coffee for your accompanying cup, or play a favorite music album. Light candles or turn on an electric fireplace. Relocate to a favorite spot indoors or out. Follow this schedule for three days. Afterward, write about what enticed you to work, and what would help you continue this practice.

CHAPTER FIVE

Taking Down Dr. Codger

"Good is the enemy of best."

—Unknown

DR. CODGER can help you work. His focus is on being responsible and punctual and regular. He is the guy who reminds you to brush your teeth every night, get to work on time and pay the bills. But since Dr. Codger thinks in black and white, he'll turn any suggestion into a rule. You've got to watch out for the subtle way he takes control. Routines can quickly become ruts, and strengths may turn into straitjackets.

Here are five ingredients to fill your life with creativity and keep you out of the same-old, same-old.

Nonsense

"We're all mad here," said the Cheshire Cat, describing the nonsense around him. No surprise then, Dr. Codger treats Wonderland as if he were the white rabbit, rushing to get away as quickly as possible. Hanging out with non-sense is good for you, though. Nonsense lets you work backwards, throwing together ingredients which normally don't mix and playing with ideas while forgetting about meanings.

Midway through the Wildfire sessions, I ask writers to empty their pock-ets and purses into a collective pile in the middle of the room. The writers study the objects and connect them any which way in a story. One class produced two photos of children, a toy block, a stapler, a cruise schedule, a cough drop, a set of playing cards, hairspray, and packet of stain remover. I asked us all to write a survival story. Here is the nonsense I wrote:

> *I sail away from Port Longview with two children on board, a stain remover and a stapler. When the high winds come, I pull out my hairspray and spray myself to the mast so I don't blow away. We have a throat lozenge to sustain us. I teach us all to play cards. When necessary, young Tommy can whistle loud and long through the hole in his grin. Vivian has a giant "A" block she can use to clobber pirates.*

Spark 1

Start writing a story backwards, last line first.

Spark 2

Outline a fantasy world with wacky rules of non-gravity, different governments, land forms, orbits, calendars, suns and moons. Create a map, complete with outlandish names.

Spark 3

In a story you're writing, throw in a bizarre character who questions everything and has completely arbitrary words and actions.

Spark 4

Play with opposites. Whatever you're working on (which for me is this book), conjure up a complete opposite, just to be zany. Here's mine.

Ice Age Scrawling: a book about how to freeze your ideas to death. Chapter Fifty-One: Making Sense. "One should strive for perfect sense at all times. If your ideas stray, destroy them immediately."

A Change of Environment

Have you ever landed somewhere new, only to find yourself acting differently? Years ago, my husband, a quiet, conservative engineer, was part of the live audience for a comedy show in Palm Springs. The entertainer randomly called him on stage for a demonstration. To his surprise and to the surprise of all his buddies with him, my husband hammed it up and began dancing with a partner onstage, dipping her in his arms like he was Fred Astaire. It wasn't alcohol, but the compelling environment which flipped his switch.

A travel guide told me about strange things that happen on his tours overseas. People form new alliances. On one of his trips, a married couple drifted apart, each attracted to someone else. It turned out the "someone elses" were married to each other. During the course of the trip, all four stayed in their new pairings. After going home, they divorced and remarried the new partners.

Far from home, the rules of life fall away. Dr. Codger loses his grip. You see a new landscape with new inhabitants. You realize that it was mere chance you were born and grew up where you did; you could be anyone at all. Your entire world can change as you examine the trappings of your existence.

The two couples took a selfish approach to this transformation, but you don't have to. Hopefully, you're more in tune with yourself than these musical-chairs partners. The point is, travel can change you. You can use it for positive, life-affirming ends.

Travel can break up tired self-concepts, jolt you into new thinking.

Leave the country. Go halfway around the world. Take a train, a boat, a plane. Go where you can be out of your depth and rely on inner resources. You'll tap new strength. You'll wake up Dream Kid.

Even if you don't travel, there are other ways to change your environment. The popularity of remodeling a home, or creating Feng Shui, speaks to the value of a new perspective. Move your desk to a new position, frame a new view.

Spark 1

Wear something dramatic, just for today. Choose a hat or scarf that isn't your typical style.

Spark 2

Take a walk down a street in a strange neighborhood.

Spark 3

Plan an outing, using different transportation than you would normally consider. Catch a taxi, ride a horse and carriage, a tram or a Greyhound bus.

Spark 4

Spend half an hour researching possible trips. Circle a month on your calendar, ten to twelve months from now, and decide when you will go.

Nature

Immersing yourself in nature is another great way to get a creative break-through. When you are overcome by the beauty of creation, it's hard to think critical thoughts. Perhaps you already have an outdoor hobby you can use for this purpose, whether gardening, bike riding, photography, sightseeing, trail running, fishing, hiking, beach combing, or walking. You may consider mountain climbing, sailing, geocaching, motorcycling, gardening, snowshoe-ing, wake boarding, rock climbing, kayaking, reading in the back yard or doing art—*en plein air*. Ride a ferry, cross a bridge. Visit an interpretive trail or an English garden. Appreciate the animal kingdom through a zoo exhibit, wildlife refuge, aquarium. When Dr. Codger is being especially meddlesome, look for the beauty of nature to refresh you, even indoors.

Spark 1

Look up national parks (www.nps.gov). Drive to the closest. Get out of your car and walk.

Spark 2

Play with your cat or dog, admire the fish in your fish tank, cull dead leaves from a houseplant.

Physical Exhaustion

Ever notice at the end of a long day of yard work or hiking or bike riding, how your mind is relaxed while your body recuperates? Intense physical activity quiets Dr. Codger in addition to promoting excellent health.

Some of my most enjoyable creative moments have been spent curled up with a journal by the fire after cross-country skiing, or soaking in the bathtub after a backpack trip. The mind is quiet and fertile while the body goes into recovery.

Spark

Plan a brainstorming session after heavy exercise. Keep your expectations low, allowing for the fact you're physically exhausted, but welcome the creative ideas.

Art and Music

As with nature, beauty jolts us out of analytical thinking and catapults us into wonder and appreciation. Choose art and music to help you get to the creative place you most need to go. Do you need to experiment? Listen to experimental music, study abstract art. Do you need discipline? Surround yourself with classics. Or, as is often the case, do you need to sink deeper into what you love, find your personal style? Then indulge your own favorites, turning up the volume on your music, not caring whether your preference is popular or current. Strew your coffee table with pictures you love. Spend a few minutes gazing at art on a restaurant wall. Go to a lawn concert. Give art and song a chance to speak to you. When they do, pay attention.

Spark 1

Take a day off and visit an art museum. Bring a sketchbook, notebook, or voice recorder and record your thoughts without any specific intention in mind.

Spark 2

Go to a local coffee shop for live music. Or stop and spend twenty minutes listening to a street musician. Connect with music being created right in front of you, raw and imperfect.

Being in Love

It's an incredible creative boost. Many of us don't feel lucky enough to keep love in our lives. Perhaps we can't find the right person, or we neglect the significant relationship we do have. We may pine for the days of early romance, or long for someone to sweep us off our feet. Regardless of your experience with love, it can and should be ignited, just like your creative fire.

For now, if you're in the midst of a passionate relationship, you are already aware of how it can infuse you with creativity and thrill, silencing Dr. Codger. Love is famous for making old people act like teenagers and making all ages ageless. Infatuation overrides our typical thinking process.

If you have ever been in love, you know how your senses seem keener, every experience heightened. At the same time, you pursue beautiful experiences with new zest—walking in a park, visiting a zoo, going to a concert.

For the element of being in love: reach out for more of life. Do the things you would do on a first date with someone you were crazy about. Do them now. Do them alone or with a long-time partner. Remember what attracted you to that person. Dream of what attracts you to the unknown future mate. Celebrate differences and venture out, seeking tantalizing experiences in the world.

Spark

Call up the feeling of falling in love. Wildwrite. What does this feeling tell you that you can do? What does this feeling tell you about yourself? Who are you as a person in love?

Opposites, Contradictions and Paradox

Tell Dr. Codger to think big and he'll rule out the small. Teach him to tell the truth, and he'll get didactic about it. He can't accept a paradox, and must always choose sides, ruling out possibilities. Since Dr. Codger can't hold two opposing ideas at the same time, this is the place where Dream Kid can thrive. Throughout this book, you'll find many paradoxes which the creative person learns to balance. A creative person needs to tell the truth, for example, but should court the ability to lie. She must be playful, but also disciplined. She has got to slow down, but must work quickly without censoring herself.

When you are faced with a problem, look at things backwards, inside out and upside down.

Yuvi Zalkow is a master at this. After years of struggling with the feeling that he was a failed writer, he surrendered to it. He made failure his platform. In his hilarious, self-deprecating way, he created a blog for writers who also struggle with failure (yuvizalkow.com). He made quirky, entertaining videos and won readers over with his honesty and kindness. At the same time, his novel, *A Brilliant Novel in the Works* (MP Publishing, 2012), found an agent, landed a publisher, and was released to many positive reviews. In short, Yuvi found success—and continues to play it down, using shame and failure as his funny, improbable path forward.

If you are trying to lose weight and having difficulty, brainstorm about what it would take for you to *gain* weight. Collect recipes that would work if you were seriously underweight and needed to pack on the pounds. Design systems for less exercise. Let your imagination run wild, but in the opposite direction of what you've been trying to accomplish.

After playing with this for half an hour or so, return to your normal position, and you'll stumble upon new ideas.

If you are having a difficult time being funny, be extremely serious. If trying to pare down a busy schedule, make it even busier. Whatever your problem, let go of it for a while and find its opposite. See what happens.

Spark 1

Wildwrite with this prompt: "Things Not Worth Writing About." With each idea you get for a writing topic, explore why it is a stupid one. Write about how it doesn't interest you. Write about how it could end up becoming an absolutely ridiculous, worthless waste of time.

Spark 2

Choose one worthless idea and call it: "The Worst Art I Will Ever Make." Now go about planning this project, as stupidly as you can.

CHAPTER SIX

Firestarters

"The sacred flame, love's beacon bright,
has been your guide and mine."

—from "Sacred Flame," a song by Will H. Heelan

AS YOU ARE GETTING your fire started, avoid wind, rain, criticism, and most of all, Dr. Codger. But watch out: Dr. Codger will hang around, throwing cold water on your lovely flames. You must persist, despite the critical thoughts that show up.

Dr. Codger is not equipped for creating, be it a story, wall mural, or theme party. Of course, with his know-it-all swagger, he'll never let on. When he's too damned uncomfortable, he'll short-circuit, shut down and leave the room. This is good.

Disable Dr. Codger so you can get on with the creating. Once you have a body of work to refine and polish, you can let him back in the room, and he'll nod and give you pointers over his clipboard. You'll need this. But for now, be willing to learn the ways to turn off this mode of thinking.

When Dr. Codger is getting uncomfortable he'll say things like:

I just can't do this.

This is a waste of time.

Skip to something else, would you?

I must not be talented or capable.

I'm not as smart as I thought.

I'm not ready yet. I need_____.

When these words come, whom do they target? You, of course. They masquerade as your thoughts. So with all the best intentions, you set out to begin your creative project and find yourself bombarded with negativity. It can be very discouraging.

Here's the secret: *the thoughts are not you.* The discomfort is a natural part of Dr. Codger's role as he fades into the background. Each thought, loaded with its little explosive cartridge, doesn't have anywhere near the power it pretends to.

You must keep writing despite the resistance.

You must accept the discomfort, the reluctance and negativity.

Trust that this will pass.

As long as you stay committed to the process, you are a writing success. This is what you must know and recognize. Simply having a negative thought does not make you a failure; the fact you don't enjoy the exercises does not mean they aren't working. In fact, quite the opposite is true. The more resistance you're feeling, the more you know you're doing the right thing. Your flames are leaping into life.

Recognize this discomfort anytime you try to break a habit or start a new one. It can happen when you sit down to say a prayer or write a love letter or step out onto the dance floor. Just because you receive negative thoughts on how it isn't working, doesn't mean these thoughts own you.

Each of the next few chapters introduces an element which will shut down Dr. Codger. You don't have to do everything, or do it all at once.

Spark

Write down something you dream of doing. Put it down on an index card, put it in your pocket, and look at it throughout the day, especially when you feel uncomfortable and vulnerable.

I am achieving my dream of _____ despite resistance.

CHAPTER SEVEN

Wildwriting

"Oh, the bright, little lantern I swing, I swing . . ."

—from a song by the same title, by Lu. B. Cake

CELLO PLAYING, quiche baking, snowboarding, bartending. Name a skill, and you'll name an activity perfected through practice. Yet for some reason we have the idea that writing is different, mystical. A true writer should pass her hand over a page and produce stunning results of sheer genius. But no. Writing takes practice, like everything else.

Wildwriting is a way to drill in daily practice, while feeding your creative fire and pushing away Dr. Codger. What it is: a mad dash of words on the page, helter skelter, messy, pointless, misspelled. It feels a little crazy. Other writing teachers have called it freewriting or speedwriting, but I like to call it wildwriting or "practice writing." It's nothing special: just practice.

The only guideline is to set a timer for ten minutes. Keep writing, no matter what drivel fills the space. What this amazing process teaches you is not to rely so heavily on thinking. As I heard once in a keynote speech by Madeleine L'Engle, late author of *A Wrinkle In Time* and numerous other books, "The mind doesn't write. The hand writes." It wasn't until I had a regular wildwriting practice that I understood what she meant.

When you start this crazy practice, Dr. Codger will most certainly complain. Some ways to cope with Dr. Codger:

- Write faster.
- Write down whatever it is Dr. Codger is telling you.
- Think: *this too shall pass.*
- Breathe. Relax as deeply as you can.
- Don't do anything.
- Keep writing.

If you wildwrite on a regular basis, you'll find shimmering breakthroughs like torches in the darkest cave. You'll also find a lot of crap.

Ignore it.

It's just part of practice.

Wildwriting will probably feel awkward and frustrating. Your discomfort is Dr. Codger, quaking in protest. When you move ahead despite the objections, he eventually gives up.

In our society, with its emphasis on results—working hard, looking successful, owning things—we feel beaten down by Dr. Codger as he tells us we're not "enough." Whenever you feel this way, wildwriting is one way to get out from underneath his rule.

Wildwriting is constrained freedom. You can say anything you like, but you don't have the liberty to sit and stare at the blank page. Instead of waiting for inspiration, you're making use of what you have this moment.

If you have been over-criticized or under-supported, wildwriting is a must. It will teach you to quit listening to the rants and barbs.

Spark

Set a timer for ten minutes. Now, wildwrite starting with this sentence: "In order to create, what I need is . . . ."

Use this prompt to explore the ways you can take care of yourself as a writer. Yet, don't worry about staying on topic. If you digress and end up writing about what you ate for breakfast, or carpet stains, or Guatemalan worry dolls, fine. The subject matter is not as important as the process of completing the exercise.

Disregard spelling, punctuation, grammar, order and every convention. Remember: this is only practice. Don't reread or cross out anything until the time is up. Take dictation from your thoughts, even, *This is ridiculous*. Go ahead and write "ridiculous," over and over until a new thought grabs you.

Something will spring up. Put it down and keep it as part of your Wildfire observations.

CHAPTER EIGHT

The Book of Fire

"I am enamored of my journal."

—Sir Walter Scott

"KEEP A JOURNAL," I tell new writing students.

"But I tried that!" they murmur, one after another with a guilty shrug. "I just can't keep it going every day." Once again, Dr. Codger is imposing rules, insisting that to write in a journal, it should be this, it should be that, and above all, it should be every day.

Strip every "should." This is not your grandmother's journal. It is not a diary of who stopped by for Sunday dinner, or your latest recipe for green bean casserole. Say what you really want and need to say. Use the principles of wildwriting. Disregard all conventions of writing learned in school. Forget complete sentences. Ignore messy handwriting.

This is your place for the naked truth, for rants and outrageous thoughts and obsessions you'd never say out loud. This is the place where change begins with the smallest idea. This is your book of fire.

It may not feature words at all. One of my clients draws in her sketchbook, taking a break from her busy day as a therapist. Your "writing" may be oil painting or prayer or dance.

Write every day. (Yep, I saw that! You cringed. Hold on a minute.) *My* suggestion to write every day won't work. However, *your* suggestion will. How do you make a self-suggestion? Give it to yourself in small, easy doses:

Mark these words on every mirror in your home: *I can do this every day.*

Buy yourself an amazing pen, fountain or gel or something in your favorite color. Use it for your journal and nothing else.

Relax, close your eyes, and imagine how great today's journal session will feel. Visualize when and where you'll journal or create art, and how gratifying this will be.

Schedule journal sessions on your calendar.

Before you go to bed at night, imagine yourself writing tomorrow.

Writing every day is an inviting possibility, not a set of handcuffs. If you skip a day, no big deal. Go on to the next day just as you would the next page, the next breath, the next step.

Stay with it. This will become a habit, and the most powerful force you have.

Whatever you do, keep coming back to the suggestion and invitation. Don't beat yourself up for failure. Don't associate this creative, open window with guilt and disappointment. It is here for you.

Spark 1

Don't buy a plush blank book festooned with inspirational quotes. Dr. Codger will scold you for writing badly and wasting it. Instead, pick a small, ratty spiral notebook with scuffed cover and wire coils bent every which way. Get a size you can carry to work, the grocery store, doctor appointments, the gym.

Waiting in line or taking a coffee break, pull out your book of fire. A good beginning is, "Today I feel . . ." or "Today I see . . . " or "I'm worried about . . . ."

Spark 2

For your art session, set aside a space. Lay out your tools and supplies neatly but visibly, where you will see and use them every day.

CHAPTER NINE

Emotional Dynamite

"My heart's all emotion, I've just formed the notion."

—from "My Sweetheart from Old Donegal," a song by George Boyden

IN TODAY'S WORLD we're at a loss for what to do with emotions. We compress them pocket-size, only taking them out in "appropriate" places. At the movies we cry or laugh; at a sports event we shout or rage; in a visit with a therapist, we talk about the feelings we never talk about. The rest of the time we keep our emotions out of sight, fearing the moment they may erupt and take control.

Our emotions are not convenient, predictable or reasonable. The beauty of writing is that it provides a safe way to explore and expose these emotions, experiencing our humanity.

Emotional dynamite will disarm Dr. Codger. It happens when you are heartsick, furious, shocked, giddy, terrified, passionate, or venting. Dr. Codger sneaks out back, embarrassed.

Here are a few different kinds of emotional dynamite. Try them, and then come up with your own.

The Holler

Some years ago, I was hiking with my best friend, fretting about the hold a broken relationship had on me. "You really need an ending," she said.

I climbed to a grassy hill and shouted at the treetops: "You can't hold me back! I'm going on with my life!" From that moment, I had a sense of power to make some hard decisions and get on with living.

Drive to a remote place. If there are people within earshot, keep your windows rolled up. Otherwise, get out and stretch your arms to the sky. Think on frustrations and disappointments, letting anger boil up. Shout out whatever words or curses show up in your mouth. Grab paper or a voice recorder and rant as long as you can about what's on your mind.

Spark

Review the stupid, pointless, heroic or crazy things you were duped into doing which kept you from your creativity. Watching TV? Babysitting your nephew? Target all your blame on an entity of your choice: Society, Dr. Codger, your Great Aunt Clementine, Satan.

You might start laughing. You might be shaking. Wildwrite for ten minutes.

The Heartbreak

Think back to a time when you were heartbroken. You may have found yourself acting totally out of character, too distraught to care. You cried in a restaurant. Or you wrote pages and pages of a letter, nonstop. Perhaps you went for a walk down a dangerous alley and didn't think twice. Intense sadness jolts us out of our everyday routine where Dr. Codger is in charge.

Spark

Call up a sad memory or thought. Dwell on a painful part of your life you don't like to think about. Don't worry, it won't kill you, even if Dr. Codger says so. Close your eyes, take a deep breath and feel the ripples of sadness in your body, the tightness in your chest, the sting of tears in the bones of your face. There will be much power to share on the page. Wildwrite for ten minutes, aiming straight for what hurts.

The Big Silly

Sometimes you act the fool and don't care. Gene Kelly soft-shoed through puddles with rivers of water trailing down his grinning face in the musical, *Singin' In the Rain*. He played Don Lockwood, who had fallen in love. Love overrode the man's circuits.

In tenth grade alone in my room I had a religious experience. I raced down the street to my friend's house. "God loves me!" I told my friend. "I mean—God really loves me!"

She squinted her eyes at me. "O-kay. Are you feeling all right?"

Can you think of a time you got good news, and the usually-quiet you shouted it to the world? Did you ever sing a love song at your desk, take the podium to say thank you, or break into laughter during a solemn meeting? Your Dream Kid was free, and Dr. Codger was powerless.

Spark

Quietly close your eyes and visualize a happy, silly moment.

How did you feel?

What made you carefree?

What does your creative soul have to say about it?

Wildwrite for ten minutes.

CHAPTER TEN

Breaking Rules

"Who dares the bronco wild defy?
Who looks the mustang in the eye?"

—from "Natoma: an Opera in Three Acts," by Joseph D. Redding

SO MANY RULES we've followed, trying to appease Dr. Codger so he'll confirm what good people we are. This doesn't work. (Tip: he doesn't give compliments.)

We follow rules in order to make a good impression, get along, gain approval. Dream Kid doesn't care about these things. Dream Kid is only interested in the play of creating.

In reality, the creative folks are those not afraid of breaking rules, trying their own theories and structures, inventing original ways of doing things. If you have found yourself in a rule-following pattern, it's time you broke some rules. As you look at the following dictums of society, go beyond the surface. Let the boldness and virtue in your core overtake your skin-deep habits of being nice, neat and polite. Find out what it really means to be good.

This will outwit Dr. Codger. Sparks will fly.

Be Nice.

In your writing, tell the truth. Say what you actually think. Tell off an annoying boss. Describe to Aunt Martha what you really did with her kitschy

Christmas present. Some of your rants may be light and silly; some may be the stuff of the heart.

The paper never needs to reach anyone's hands in order to reach the truth.

Call names, make accusations, be ugly. Hold pity parties, throw temper tantrums, pout. Talk about friends behind their backs. Grab your journal, put your elbows on the table, and talk with your mouth full.

Spark

Think of someone you've always wanted to tell off. Imagine the conversation: the look on her face, your own posture standing tall, your words coming out loud and clear. Write your conversation in a dialogue or play script.

Don't Make a Mess.

Creativity means making mistakes. You can be dimwitted or a total flop. Your wildfire can't be hurt by any mess you make.

One Wildfire student, Jeremy, shared a story that appeared in the book, *Art and Fear*, by David Bayles and Ted Orland. A pottery instructor divided his class into two groups. He told the first group he was going to grade them on quality. It didn't matter how many pieces they threw, as long as their finished work was close to perfect.

To the second group, he said that he would grade on quantity. Their pieces could be horrible; he didn't care. He just wanted them to make as many pots as possible.

Jeremy asked, "Where do you think the best quality in that class came from?"

After a moment, our class guessed right. The pottery students who threw messy pots any which way, over and over again, were the students who created the most beautiful pieces. Freedom to make messes means you can practice and free up your creator.

As scriptwriters Blake Edwards and Larry Gelbart wrote, providing the line for Fred Astaire in *The Notorious Landlady*, "The higher up you go, the more mistakes you are allowed. Right at the top, if you make enough of them, it's considered to be your style."

In high school, my aunt gave me a burgundy velour journal for Christmas, along with a calligraphy set. I never felt comfortable scribbling my crooked letters into this gorgeous book. Instead, I splattered my lettering attempts on old envelopes, phone books, notepads. The velour journal remained beautiful—and empty—for years. I didn't know how to pull out the stops and mess up something perfect.

Spark

Scratch down some huge, sloppy letters. Write illegibly. If you're right-handed explore the scrawl of your left hand, or vise-versa. Bring messy, happy creativity into mundane things: grocery lists, calendars, table-settings, the way you answer the telephone.

Do Your Best.

This sweet-faced saying can do more harm than good. Twin sister to it is the saying, "Anything worth doing is worth doing well."

Donna Jo Napoli, prolific fantasy author, was able to write seven books while working full time *and* raising five children. She also kept a garden and participated in a writing group. Speaking at a conference of children's writers, she said, "Raising children, writing, career, they're important. But many things are barely worth doing. And if something is barely worth doing, I barely do it!" She understood how to give herself freedom.

Instead of putting forth tremendous effort for every little thing, pick and choose. Dr. Codger will get on your case and call you a slacker. But Dream Kid needs you to let go of some doings. She needs space to create, not worrying about "best effort."

When tasks are not all that important (Housework? Your shopping list? Tuesday's lunch?) tackle them with shameless nonchalance. And when it comes to writing, don't let the "quality of your work" get in the way of attempting something big. Your life and talent are too important for you to hold back for the sake of fussy details.

Spark

Do something you've never tried because you insisted it had to be done well. Write a sonnet, bake a soufflé, or have those new friends over to the house—without cleaning.

Put Others First.

This is the sneakiest rule of all. The problem with putting others first is we don't understand how to do so. We see only the short term, not the broad view. We actually do damage by tending to the urgent, visible needs of others over our own well-being. Yes, we should serve our fellow humans. You can't serve others, however, if you don't take care of yourself.

My car needs oil changes, tune ups, quality fuel and protection from the elements. If I don't provide these things for my car, it will deteriorate. I may insist on "putting others first." My family may cry out, "We need to get to work, school, the dentist, the mall, for heaven's sake!" But if I don't stop and take time to properly care for my vehicle, I won't be able to drive it three feet.

In the same way, I need physical, spiritual and emotional care in order to function. If this is provided, I can serve more folks, and with more energy, smoothly humming along instead of getting stranded by the roadside. By putting self first, I really *am* putting others first.

Pay attention to what matters to you. This is how you can serve the world. Your art is one of those priorities.

Spark

Pass on a volunteer commitment, or hand off a task to someone else, so that you can spend the time creating.

CHAPTER ELEVEN

Tinder Memories

"Some memories are realities, and are better than anything
that can ever happen to one again."

—Willa Cather, *My Antonia*

THINK BACK to the best and worst experiences of your life. There's a burst of fuel that will propel your work forward with depth, experience, emotion, and character.

This can be most challenging, though, when the memories are ones you'd rather not remember. I've been asked many times, "Isn't writing a difficult memory reopening an old wound?"

Yes, but your most powerful stories are the ones that have brought pain. Honoring those stories is a kind of healing. After thirty years, I gained the courage to write about a troubled childhood with my birth mother. Emotions were churned up; I felt raw and vulnerable and there was a bleakness that came over my life like a cloud. It took honesty and courage to keep writing about the past.

After several months writing my memories, I no longer felt weird for the way I grew up; in fact, I found it easier to relate to people. I experienced an upwelling of forgiveness for others, a greater understanding of myself. The stories of my life took on a different hue. They were no longer happy or sad but richly toned, like a beautiful painting.

My childhood ceased to be a dark memory and became a living force. It supplied me with ideas and inspirations, poems and short stories, essays and novels.

Writing about the past can bring you into the present. When you open your mind to the memory, experiencing it in the *now*, you gain peace, wisdom, and creative insight.

Remove all your judgments about what happened as you travel back through time with your imagination. Become the young adult or child that you were. Relive the adventures, disasters, trials and triumphs.

Spark 1

Here are number of ways you can work with your memories.

- Write down your most embarrassing experience. Laugh at the funny parts.
- Make photocopies (or use originals) of pictures painful to look at. Afterward, rip and tear your entries and photos. Paste them on posterboard. Add contrasting words and images from magazines. Make a collage of all these shredded bits and pieces.
- Write a personal memory as a short story. Combine real people into composite characters, or change the names.
- Try writing from the perspective of a character besides yourself. Write about someone you don't sympathize with.

Spark 2

One Hundred Memories. Write them in any order you like. Or paint or draw or sculpt them, bringing the memories into the present moment. Or try writing them in present tense.

1. The first time I ever saw the ocean
2. A trip to the zoo
3. A family vacation
4. A memorable or not-so-memorable Christmas
5. A pet that meant something to me
6. My first boyfriend (or girlfriend)
7. An accident, stitches or surgery
8. Something I did that surprised me or others
9. My first car
10. A wilderness adventure
11. A bad hotel stay
12. An odd or eccentric person in my life
13. My first date, first kiss, or other romantic experience
14. An experience on stage
15. A family joke
16. Something I have a special talent for
17. A recipe I've perfected—or a burnt barbecue or disaster dish
18. My favorite color, and why, and if it has ever changed
19. Something a parent did for me
20. Something I wish my parent(s) had done for me
21. A trip I've taken
22. A proud moment
23. A memory of rain
24. An ambition I had as a child
25. A toy I remember

26. A favorite hiding place

27. Three best friends, and what they mean or meant

28. A trait I love about myself

29. What my cat or dog would say if it could talk

30. A boss I loved (or hated)

31. A childhood fear (barking dogs, the dark, etc.)

32. The hardest thing I ever did

33. The easiest thing I ever did

34. Favorite form of exercise

35. Three to five favorite books, and why

36. Favorite ethnic dish or restaurant

37. A person who makes me laugh

38. A time I was proud to be in my family

39. Lessons I took, and how that turned out

40. A friend I lost

41. Favorite season of the year

42. A silly fear

43. Something nobody knows about me

44. My favorite outfit, and why

45. Something everybody knows about me

46. A strange neighbor

47. Someone I formed an opinion of, who completely changed my mind

48. A collection I started

49. A family heirloom

50. A memory that turns my stomach

51. A failed attempt at something

52. An experiment that produced an unexpected result

53. Three qualities I value in a friend (or mate)

54. Something I'd invent if I got around to it

55. Why I'm a good (or bad) driver

56. How I feel about housework/yardwork

57. My favorite tool in the garage

58. What I want to do when I retire

59. The famous person I'd like most to meet

60. A story from my life with the color red in it

61. Snow

62. A movie I love

63. A big mistake I made

64. The smartest thing I ever did

65. A conversation I'd like to have

66. A story from my life with the color blue in it

67. Something I'm excited about

68. The first time I ever saw my child (grandchild, niece, etc.)

69. A trip to the beach

70. A solo vacation

71. A frightening Halloween

72. An annoying pet

73. My last boyfriend (or girlfriend)

74. A narrow escape

75. A habit I broke

76. My first (or special) doll (or action figure)

77. A city trip

78. A bad camping trip

79. The most predictable person in my life

80. My first crush

81. A time when I ran away from responsibility

82. A proud moment

83. Something I don't have a talent for

84. Something I wish I could cook like Mom

85. Colors in my home

86. A thing I had to do for myself

87. A special gift

88. The house in which I lived the longest

89. Something I'm ashamed of

90. A memory of snow

91. An ambition I had as a teenager

92. A toy or game I invented with make-do objects

93. Making dirt or mud pies

94. Someone I wish I could see again, and why

95. Another trait I love about myself

96. What my plants or yard or garden would tell me if they could

97. My favorite thing to do as a teenager

98. A time I said no

99. A shot in the dark that worked

100. A story with wind, kites or gales

Spark 3

Starting with the truth, fictionalize any of these memories. Write from the point of view of a character other than yourself. Try writing in first, second or third person.

Spark 4

Fabricate the stories purely from your imagination. Let them be as outlandish as you like.

CHAPTER TWELVE

Flaming Targets

"Here's what's wrong with you.
After you get what you want you don't want it"

—from a song by the same title, by Irving Berlin

"WRITE DOWN your goals!" barked the motivational speaker. "Set deadlines for each one!"

I dutifully jotted my answers on the glossy worksheet with the seminar logo. All around me, people were promising themselves, "I'm going to make this much money in twelve months," or "I'm going to lose *x* amount of weight by April 1."

I heard this urging many times, in many different settings. Always, I would obey the motivational guru, putting together a plan with those hailed *action steps.*

I would set a goal to buy a car, specifying year, make and model. I would put down salary figures. I would sketch a new house.

Later, on, I would lose interest in all of these goals. Then, a few years ago, I realized what was wrong with my goal setting technique. I was pushing myself to go for desires that weren't in my heart.

I had to ask myself: What was I dreaming of? Writing my stories and championing the creative process and watching others' eyes light up.

I've learned there is a big difference between what you *think* you want, and what you *truly* want. And if you consult Dr. Codger, you'll get the surface view of what you want, but not the deep-down truth.

The problem is, when you get the pseudo-desire, you're not happy. It's fun for a while, but then it becomes just another thing, relationship, achievement, whatever.

We whip out proclamations or New Year's Resolutions or writing schedules, but they don't resonate.

The truth of your desires is nested in your soul. Time and patience and quiet can bring them to the surface. Chances are, what you want the most in the world is not something easily expressed. It doesn't figure into a plan or show on a chart. Your challenge is to reach into those shadowy, nonverbal spaces and find out what breaks you open.

Your brightest longings will stir you deeply; they aren't about external rewards.

In short, goals are important, but they can't be produced off the cuff.

That's the first thing you need to know about goals. The second thing is this: When creative people finally figure out where they want to go, they have a special ability to get there.

In *The Handbook of Creativity*, by John A. Glover, Royce R. Ronning and Cecil R. Reynolds, the authors explain that the difference between an "ordinary" person and a creative achiever has to do with motivation. Creative people know their targets.

Although faced with many challenges, creative individuals find it in themselves to persist over long periods of time until at last they achieve the goals they believe in.

Think "vision" or "purpose" instead of "goal." Rather than pick your goal out of a hat, think about it for weeks, months. What do you really want?

You must know where you're headed and what you hope for. When you ask for specific things that are true desires of your heart, they can happen. On the other hand, when you approach life with vague wishes, the way most people do, you'll get vague results.

When I want to see where I'm headed, I start with Dream Kid, not Dr. Codger. I start with dreams.

Many of us gave up our childhood dreams like outgrown toys. Yet they hold the key to what you really wanted from life. What were the secret ambitions you had as a child? What dreams would you dream if anything were possible?

Think about your purpose. As Eric Liddell (played by Ian Charleson) said in the movie, *Chariots of Fire*, "*I believe that God made me for a purpose, but he also made me fast. When I run, I feel his pleasure.*" When do you feel God's pleasure?

To be sure of where I want to go, I have to ask some big questions.

- *What fulfills me?*
- *What do I get out of creating? (Writing, painting, filmmaking, singing, acting, choreographing, etc.)*
- *What do I hope to give others through creating?*
- *How do I want to influence friends, family and neighbors?*
- *What can I teach the world?*
- *Who do I want to touch?*
- *How can I make my greatest impact?*
- *What's the most thrilling thing I can think of?*
- *How can I make the world a better place for my great grandchildren?*
- *What was I born to create?*
- *What's my story?*
- *What are my best gifts?*
- *Who are the people I have been especially given to?*
- *How can I make a difference right where I live?*
- *What truth do I return to, again and again?*
- *How do I bring joy to others?*
- *How do I want to be remembered?*

Wildwrite about any and all of these questions. Take an afternoon off, without phone or computer, and think about your life. When you visit your desires and purposes daily, monthly, yearly, they grow in shape and focus. They steer you in amazing ways.

I was delighted to discover the approach of one artist, Lisa Sonora Beam, through her blog at www.lisasonora.com. Author of *The Creative Entrepreneur*, she suggests that goals be set year by year, starting with an overarching theme—Clarity, Balance, Focus, Productivity—you name it. Now pick categories for your goals, depending on what's important to you. You might include wellness, finances, friendships, marriage, work, faith community, family, and learning. Next, Beam suggests a review of the past year, reflecting on what has worked in each category. She offers the question, "If I were to focus on just one thing in this category that would make the biggest difference in my life by this time next year, what would I choose?"

My favorite thing about Beam's work is that she understands the creative person's need for visuals. No more boring black leather. She teaches how to design your own Creative Planner, thick with visual reminders and prompts, textured with beautiful handmade papers.

Hunt through magazines for images that support your desires for the year. Paste them onto cardboard or canvas, creating a vision board. Even more fun: do this with people you feel a kinship with. My group of women friends still talks about the vision boards we made a couple years ago. We were so excited when these things started unfolding in one another's lives.

Spark 1

Make a list of everything you wanted to be when you were a kid, from sculptor to actor to NBA player. Take one of these roles and write yourself into a fantasy scene where you've achieved your ambition.

Spark 2

What are you dreaming but afraid to start? Complete this sentence: *If I could create anything and not fail, I would create...*

Spark 3

Schedule four times a year when you will review the above big questions about where you're going. Write these dates on the calendar and do whatever you can to make them happen.

Spark 4

Make creative visuals for your goals. They're dreams with dates. I have one goal that swings from my dining room light. It's a painted disk—decorated with red glitter swirls and the title of my next novel.

Hang a creative reminder from a lamp, rear view mirror or doorframe. Make yourself a necklace, plaque, insignia. Write the goal in gorgeous font and save it as your computer wallpaper.

Spark 5

Share a goal with a trusted partner. If you don't have a trusted partner, make it a goal to find one. Join a creative association or writers group. Go to a workshop or retreat in your creative field. Hook up online or in person with someone who shares your outlook.

CHAPTER THIRTEEN

Roughing It

"As on we go through life's career,
how many have to rough it."

—from "I Will Stand by My Friend," a song by Bedford Reuter

IF YOU BUILD A FIRE and let it burn free, you'll get uncomfortable. That's a fact. Somewhere we got the idea that the creative experience should be sweet and sunny. But as your wildfire burns, you'll feel more like squirming than celebrating.

When I've been busy with Dr. Codger's lists of things to do, welcoming back the Dream Kid is difficult. I'm in control, clean and cool. I know that once I give way to the fire, I'll be covered head to toe in soot, smoke and sweat. I won't be in charge anymore.

It's always the worst, and the best, after that fire gets started. I'm surrounded by clutter, haphazard meals, and pockets of chaos. In the work itself, outlines are trashed as compositions shape themselves in new ways. Characters stare me down with hands on hips and say, "You want me to do that? No way. I'm not budging." I have no idea what might happen next.

I step away and put things in order, only to face the fact that once again the world will blur and shift around me like smoke. I feel lost. It's all such a *bother!* But when I stop protesting, that raging, beautiful wildfire is allowed to do its work.

We need to allow discomfort. When we do, Dr. Codger leaves the picture and we find a new kind of peace independent of circumstances and environment. We can shape, draw, write, create, and be ourselves. Dream Kid thrives in an imperfect world.

Spark

Think of all the uncomfortable things you have to face in order to embrace your creativity. Draw a line down the middle of a page, and on the left side, describe the feelings, sensations and experiences. On the right side, write the hard facts and logical reasons you need to write. List everything that pulls you into the creative process, despite how you feel about it.

CHAPTER FOURTEEN

Catch Your Breath

"Breathe, oh! Breathe that strain again."

—from "Softly, Lightly, Sweetly Sing," a song by T.M. Newton

TO DISCOVER ONE'S BREATH is a wonder. I take a breath and a moment later do so again. The amazing thing about breath is: there will always be another, as long as I live.

Who takes a breath and judges it? "Darn--that was a horrible breath! I really did terribly on that breath." That would be ridiculous, of course. So it is with our writing. You write one word and let it go. Another is coming along any second. You welcome each word, a breath of air here and gone, serving its purpose until you reach for the next.

Breathing and creating are connected. Breathing fills your body with nourishment, relaxes and enlivens you. When you breathe well, you create well.

The first time I tried breathing before writing, I wrote: *What I realize is I am not breathing enough, that ideas are as close as my next breath, or as far as the breath I'm not allowing myself to take. Too busy to breathe? Too busy to take in more life? If I don't have time to breathe, I'm dying in a small way.*

Spark

Close your eyes and enjoy the experience of breathing deeply for five minutes. Feel your ribcage expand as you sit tall. Exhale slowly, letting each breath dissolve into the air around you. As you begin to write, notice how the rhythm of your breathing is a gentle backdrop and how your thoughts unfold with ease.

CHAPTER FIFTEEN

The Gaze

"On your beauty let me gaze."

—from "Happy Faces, A Ballad," by Thos. Haynes Bayly, Esq.

THERE ARE TIMES we do much more than look. We lose ourselves. We seem to be memorizing the contours of the image we love. If looking at another person, we consume this being with our eyes. The object of our attention might be a sunset, a beloved pet, a newborn baby, a lover, an intimate friend, a parent, a wild deer visiting our back yard. We might be embracing someone or standing on a hilltop or holding a hand at a bedside. Under such a look, all details speak beauty and rightness—even the face of a scarred child or the liver-spotted hand of an elderly relative. "Beauty" is no longer the media standard. It has nothing to do with perfection as society knows it. With such a gaze, even imperfections contribute to the loveliness.

This gaze is Dream Kid's way of loving the world. She takes in the scene, deeply "breathing" it through her senses. For writers, artists and creators, gazing brings glory to life.

Rick Guidotti is someone who has learned the value of gazing. A former high-fashion photographer, Rick devotes himself to photographing people with genetic conditions such as albinism, Sturge-Weber syndrome, and many others. Because he can gaze with the eyes of Dream Kid, Rick is able to see the beauty and magic in bodies and faces society would label disfigured, ugly or strange. His gazing has enabled him to photograph people all over the world and has led him to found Positive Exposure (www.positiveexposure.org), an organization supporting human dignity. Indeed, the power of gazing can change the world.

When I was ten, my camp counselor, Peter, took several campers on a hike through the woods. A mile down the trail we stopped. "Look up at the trees," Peter said. "But *see different*. Squint your eyes to get that hazy sight. Now everything will be magic." The light spangled and played through the branches, a dazzling skyscape.

While I was off at camp, learning this new way of looking, my grandmother was making the difficult decision to place me in foster care. My family was torn apart by mental illness. For practical purposes, I was orphaned. Yet I would emerge into adulthood as a believer in humanity, in God, and in myself. My ability to "see different," to find the positives in a negative world, helped me through rough times.

Why don't we use the gaze? We're in too much of a hurry. We make our plans and hold them tightly. We don't want to get distracted, and gazing is terribly distracting. In a way I was lucky: experiencing a difficult life event can catapult a person into seeing the world differently. If everything is humming along just fine, however, we tend to keep doing what seems to be working.

Gazing can take you in an entirely new direction. For Rick Guidotti, en route to Milan in his high-profile career, the day he gazed at a young albino girl at a bus stop, his future was altered forever. "The gorgeous kid waiting for the bus wasn't odd or unappealing or drab," he says. "She was amazing. All these stunning kids are. It's about steadying your gaze long enough to see, to revel, to be thrilled by unique beauty."

Make the shift. Trust yourself to see beauty no one else has discovered.

Spark 1

Spend some time gazing at a person or animal or piece of nature that you love. Can you see something you've never noticed before? Write about it.

Spark 2

Look around you and find something drab or ugly at first glance. It might be a scraggly plant wintering in your garden, a mud puddle alongside your driveway, or a moth clinging to your back door screen. Gaze for five minutes. Take a photograph or wildwrite what you see.

CHAPTER SIXTEEN

Ignore It

"Who was it? Tell me! You forget?
Oh! As if you did not know."

—from "As If You Didn't Know," a song by J.T. Gosden

THERE ARE TIMES when gazing will seriously impede you. You could get in a car accident and destroy your own future or someone else's. You could earn yourself an enemy in a crowded bar. You could mortify your teenage offspring. So while a creator must gaze and absorb nuances, he can't do so in all circumstances. In order to reach your goals, you must ignore some stimuli. Here are things I'm ignoring at this moment:

- Today's date, December 10. I haven't started my Christmas shopping.
- A pile of clean laundry sitting on top of the dryer.
- A client's book I must edit this afternoon.
- The Internet. I've already been sucked into it once today.
- A cranberry scone recipe that wants baking.
- The clock.
- A phone call I haven't returned and an RSVP I haven't made.
- Lint on my bathroom floor.
- The need to raise the blinds, wash last night's dishes, wash my hair.
- My blog, where I haven't posted for a month.

None of these things demands my attention unless I let it. I have chosen to work on my book instead. Yet, I know other creators who don't take time for their creating until every last thing is done. I've played this game, and it's endless because the little things never end.

Ignoring is a wonderful skill. Many of us are equipped with a tremendous ability to ignore. One writer worked in a health care office surrounded by patients and caregivers coming and going. She tried to write in a quiet space, but this didn't work. She found that ignoring gave her strength. Now she writes in the noisiest coffee shop in town.

Unfortunately, most of us have misused our talent for ignoring. We've ignored the wrong things. We've ignored our creative ideas, our incubating time, and our talents. Take that ability to block out interruptions and close off side trails. Use it to your benefit.

Spark 1

You are probably ignoring something as you read this. Take a moment and look around you. Can you see what it is what you've blocked out so effectively?

Spark 2

Make a list of things you can and should ignore this week, in order to accomplish a creative goal.

CHAPTER SEVENTEEN

Burned Down to the Truth

"Fiction is the lie that tells the truth truer."

—Tom Spanbauer

TOM SPANBAUER, acclaimed writing teacher and author of *Now is the Hour* and other novels, told the story of growing up confused and isolated in an ultra-conservative small town. He shared with the students at Haystack Program in the Arts (July 2003) how he was beleaguered as a teenager by a multitude of voices telling him what to think. Then he began keeping his Truth Book. In it he could write the truth of what he saw and felt, making an honest observation such as, "Sally came back from summer vacation with really big breasts," or "Why does the school nurse look at the floor when she's talking to the principal?" Telling the truth taught him to listen to himself, believe in his own observations and ideas, and become an award-winning novelist.

I was lucky enough to take a fiction workshop from Tom several years ago. He challenged me and the rest of the class to go to the truths in the story that most folks skip over, using simple language to show even the most harrowing, painful, or unthinkable details—this he termed "Dangerous Writing."

And yes, the truth is dangerous. But along with that danger, truth brings beauty, too, and even love.

There are many truths in our culture which we are afraid of. A few of these:

Science doesn't have all the answers.

Everyone I love will die.

I have made mistakes that hurt others.

My life is for a limited time.

I will fail at some things.

Truth energizes you; gives you something to say that's worthwhile. Writing which avoids truth is tired and limp and full of cliché. Clichés are easy, quick and safe. When we repeat someone else's truth, we recycle phrases and we don't have to take the risk of opening to our own truths.

We need to examine the world through our own eyes. As writers and creators we summon our opinions, responses and reactions to people, objects, things and events—and then we tell the truth about them.

If I report, "it's raining cats and dogs," I haven't looked at the rain, really. I'm just noting the fact that it's raining. But if I stop what I'm doing, getting up from my desk—now—slipping on my shoes to go out the back door, I can stand in the rain and experience it. Here is the rain, much lighter than I thought. I can hear the gutters gurgling. It's raining on my head, soft pinpricks. Those soft pinpricks are the truth; the cats and dogs are not. Except, perhaps, for the first person who said it.

Many things are tricky to describe or difficult to look at, and so we resort to these clichés. Eyes: "Her eyes twinkled." Dying: "biting the dust," or "breathing his last." Hearts, which we can't physically see: "His heart was pounding," or "Her heart was in her throat."

When we undertake art, we are confronted with the fact we don't see the world correctly. In learning to draw a face, my first attempt was an easy, trite image, a cartoon face. It was all wrong. But I persisted, broke through the old way of seeing, and finally recognized much of the area I'd ignored was an important part of the face: the forehead, the sides of the jaw, and the planes around the ears. Only when I saw the face with Dream Kid vision, could I bring it to paper. As my watercolor teacher, Lee Baugham, says, "If you can't see it, you can't paint it."

In the same way, if you can't see it, you can't write it. Especially in fiction, for in fiction we create stories we haven't seen physically, but must visualize clearly.

Imagination is the most important ingredient for the storyteller. Here's how it becomes true: slow down and absorb the scene through your senses. Play it in your mind. Your imagination will take you places that don't coincide with the facts.

A lie about facts, when telling a story, can be closer to the truth than something half-imagined. Especially when the truth becomes worn and tired and unnoticed: nothing but recycled words.

As the late George Carlin pointed out in his HBO special *Doin' It Again* (1990), "Americans have trouble facing the truth, so they invent a kind of soft language to protect themselves from it."

In 2009, when the recession began, political voices said this country was experiencing "economic downturn." Finally, mid-2010, the words "Great Recession" came up. Yet even if things get as bad economically as they were in 1930, the media won't be calling it a depression.

I worked on a church newsletter several years ago, and would list the names of people who died that week. "Never mind all that 'passed away' stuff," said Becki, the savvy program manager. "It's clearer and truer just to say they died." Thank goodness for her insight. Certainly there were families and friends who were grieving, but words like "passed away" or "dearly departed," or "no longer with us," were not going to alleviate their sadness.

Yet it feels safer to use euphemisms and clichés. Dr. Codger convinces us it sounds better. These snappy phrases have an economy; for example, "twinkling eyes." But what you gain in truth is far better than what you lose in finesse. In the end I might simply say, "She had beautiful green eyes. They were full of light." Telling the truth can make you stumble. It will seem awkward. It may take more words. I experienced this a moment ago, standing at the back door trying to describe the rain.

Spark 1

Make a list of interesting emotions, such as curiosity, excitement, fear, loneliness, disgust, pride, and relief. With a partner, take turns acting out an emotion while the other writes about it without benefit of knowing the chosen word.

The actor can use his face or whole body to express the particular feeling, while the partner observes and writes about it. In describing the actor, can you show the lines of the face, the posture, the movements? How can you describe the eyes? Can you show what you see, without having to name the exact emotion?

Option: You can do this in a group, with players drawing the emotions from a hat and acting them out in turn.

Spark 2

Find a "trouble spot" in something you are writing, drawing or painting, that you can't quite visualize. Have a friend model it for you, whether it's your protagonist shaking hands with the president, or a woman crossing her arms in defiance. What would this really look like? See if you can find out.

CHAPTER EIGHTEEN

Lying Tongues

"There are three types of lies—
lies, damn lies, and statistics."

—Leonard H. Courtney in a New York speech, 1895

A LYING CHILD is said to be one who "tells stories." The word *lie* seems stark and evil, while telling stories has always appealed to me. It's a good thing no one called my childhood lies stories, or I would have thought this was praise. I'd have lied at every chance.

Because kids do. They lie. Dream Kid enjoys a good lie as well. There is something amazing and delightful about convincing someone of something that isn't true. The really good liars know how to use just enough truth in their lies, enough heartfelt emotion, to convince you they're telling the truth.

The best way to lie in your art is with the surface details: the when, where and how. The juxtapositions. Adding a tree to the painting of a river. Or taking away a character from a biography who wasn't integral to the story. Or melding two characters from a memoir into one. Changing the lighting in a photograph. All of these could be seen as "lying" to the Dr. Codger mind. They are all ways of telling stories.

Many of us have gotten so used to Dr. Codger's false morality that we've lost the ability to spin a really good yarn, to embellish an anecdote, or to deviate from "what was actually there" when creating art from nature or real life. We were so shamed by our lies that we lost the ability to lie in the juicy, delightful ways that will enrich our experience.

There are, in fact, a few lies that have been embraced by our culture. Think of the lies we tell the guest of honor when planning a surprise party. Or the stories we tell children about Santa Claus. Or the lies we might tell a young child about what happened to the pet we took to the pound. These are the last bastion of creative lying.

Bald-faced lying is not a good character trait, and, naturally, we don't want to lie blatantly every day. We learned as children that lying can have painful consequences. But when it comes to creating, there's a thrill in going beyond what appears "true" at first glance. Without this thrill, where would scientists be? They must question the apparent truth in order to dig deeper. The same holds true for science fiction writers, dancers, composers. We have to question assumptions. We must jump ahead and make our own truth by leaping to the lie.

I've met some writers who invariably panic at the idea of embellishing details in a memoir scene, or making up dialogue. Accurate dialogue in memoir-writing is an utter impossibility anyway, when you think about it. We didn't carry a reporter's pad or voice recorder through all those pivotal moments of our lives. It takes courage to lie: to create the story in rich detail to engage our reader or viewer.

As my high school oil painting teacher told me, "Real life is boring. Art gives us the chance to recreate it." In the process of creating art, we "lie" by brightening the colors, painting the sky crimson and flamingo. In real life, it was just another pretty sunset. Giving ourselves permission to lie unleashes the imagination.

Spark 1

Remember the first delicious lie you ever told. What was the story? Who believed it?

Spark 2

This is a Wildfire adaptation of the party game "Two Truths and A Lie." For the version I use in class, I have each player write down ten facts about him or herself. Some may be true and some fabricated. These can be facts of any kind: accomplishments, family, birthplace, vocation, likes or dislikes. When the lists are completed each player reads his list, and the rest of the class votes on what they believe true and what they believe false. It's great fun with a roomful of creators who use quirky, believable details and know how to fool a crowd.

Spark 3

Break out the Balderdash board game. Based on the parlor game, "Dictionary," this game involves making up false definitions for obscure, little-known words. Use your professorial tone and your most authoritative voice and see how well you can fib.

CHAPTER NINETEEN

Fired Up for the Journey

"[L]ove the journey, God is with you,
come home safe and sound."

—Anne Lamott, *Traveling Mercies*

NOW I'M GOING TO mix all my metaphors, take you away from the fire of creating and place you on a journey.

This journey has its own wildness. It is fluid, not linear; dynamic rather than static and staid. You can't flick your paintbrush and call it finished art. You can't whip out a sentence and call it a publishable poem. Your approach constantly changes as you shift between Dream Kid mode and Dr. Codger mode. And that's as it should be. If you don't appreciate this journey, however, you can get frustrated, confused, sidetracked. You can rush your creativity and question your abilities. Take this virtual road trip with me cocreated by teacher extraordinaire, Nancy Fertig of Battleground, Washington.

The Creative Journey

Station One: The Playground

Creativity doesn't begin in a vacuum, prison camp, or labor yard. It begins when you have an idea. And when you have an idea, even for a moment, you're in a creative playground.

Ever watch kids on a playground? They are relaxed and free, not thinking about anything but having fun. Racing from merry-go-round to jungle gym to tire swing. A playground is a place for enjoying, not perfection. Typically, kids don't dress up to go to a playground. They don't wear their dress-up best. Think about it. How do you approach your writing? Be a kid in play clothes, relaxed and easy, ready to have fun.

Ideas come when people are relaxed. Athletes achieve most in this state, which allows maximum oxygenation. By contrast, stress and tension will limit performance and staunch the flow of ideas. No matter how you grit your teeth, ideas won't come when you're trying too hard.

Being in the playground may mean going for a walk, reading a book, visiting an art gallery, taking a trip, hiking in the wilderness, having a picnic. As you begin, you reflect about what you're going to create. Even simple daily activities such as driving the car or taking a shower can be relaxed moments of Playground creation. You'll know by the way thoughts and ideas come to you.

Taking it one step further, the Playground may mean doing research, creating an outline, making a rough sketch of the project. You are still in the beginning stage, trying the idea on for size.

The Playground is the place where ideas have their beginnings. They playfully sneak up and tap you on the shoulder, then run and tease you to beat them to the last swing. When the journey involves writing, I call this station the Playground of Prewriting.

The creative process requires not just one idea, but many. Writing a story, for example, you'll need an idea of what happens, who the characters are, and where the story takes place. You'll need to identify the main conflict, and target each character's traits. You'll need an idea about what time period the story happens in. Now, you don't need all of these ideas in the beginning. Many don't occur until the work is underway. But if you know the ins and outs of the Playground, you know where to get the ideas.

The Playground is Dream Kid's turf. It's never cool for an adult to come onto the scene and say, "Dumb idea," or "Beat it, kid." The Playground of Prewriting is off-limits to curmudgeons.

Going to the Playground can mean taking an actual trip to the beach or the zoo, anywhere that inspires you. Julia Cameron, author and founder of *The Artist's Way*, calls this an "artist date." The artist needs a place to treat herself, stimulating the process of creating. More than a luxury, it's a necessity.

When you visualize a work, understand that the idea is the very beginning, and the environment which produces ideas is all important. This is why you establish yourself in this joyful, easy place. Not to say that you can't get a heartbreaking idea, or be unhappy while you create, but in spite of your mood, there is a little shot of joy when that idea lands on you, light and free like a butterfly on your hand. For many of us, it's the reason we create in the first place.

Station Two: Draft Camp

You get back in your car and tool down the road a piece. Before you lies the open road. Soon you'll see signs for the campground. Pull over, drive through the trees, take the left fork. Now you'll encounter campsite after campsite. Draft Camp is the place where you make a decision: *Here's where I'm going to camp out.*

Of all your ideas, thrown and tossed like Frisbees on the Playground, choose one. Make a commitment to this particular idea; you're going to stay with it. In camping, you risk rain and cold and all kinds of discomfort in the hope that this could be the best adventure of your life. It could also be the worst.

Wear your grubbies. What's the point of makeup or clean white sneakers while camping? Just make sure you're dressed warmly enough to stay awhile.

Things here are accomplished roughly. When camping, you don't scrub and sanitize your dishes. You do what you can with a squirt of camp suds. You don't cook gourmet. You don't snooze on a queen-sized Beauty Rest.

The best campers keep things simple; they don't try to bring everything they've ever owned.

There is much you'll leave behind. There will be a time for the luxury of details later on. Focus on what's before you this moment, no matter how rough.

Last week, one of my writing students became frustrated while writing a short story. He suddenly realized he'd gone into third person after starting in first. He said, "Drat! (or more savory words to that effect) I've gotten so far and here I am mixing up my persons."

Yet no experienced camper gets angry at having to make toast over a campfire instead of in a toaster. Instead of getting frustrated over your mistakes, remind yourself this is the rough version. Your tools aren't perfect but they'll get the job done.

Draft Camp lets you experiment, trying out new colors, textures, voices, persons, tenses.

Later, you'll clean up, get a good home-cooked meal and wash your hair. For now, the most important thing is that you keep going. In writing, it's fine even if you don't use complete sentences. In painting, this is only the first layer.

Pitch your tent for as long as you need. Realize that your perceptions may change again and again. But whatever happens in Draft Camp is meant to happen. It is never a waste of time.

Flesh out your work. You may have sketches, outlines or other devices you brought from the Playground. But you have to surrender to the fact you can't know exactly how things will turn out.

Don't correct your mistakes. Stay in Draft Camp without rushing to the next part. Too often, creators can't live with their mistakes and the ambiguity of it all. They're dying to know about the final product. Will it be worthwhile?

I'm always amused by beginning writers who rush this stage. They are like children who want to go to Disneyland but don't want to ride in the car that long. One writer said, "Here. Read my first chapter. Just tell me if it's any good, and if I have any talent, because I want to know now before I waste any more time."

Dr. Codger loves this attitude: he calls it efficiency. But in a backwards way, it's creative laziness. You have no idea how good you are until you give the work your best strength. It may take years before you see your talents emerging in reality. Don't reserve your energy "just in case" your work is no good. As Annie Dillard compels us in *The Writing Life*, "spend it all, shoot it, play it, lose it, all . . . ."

Draft Camp is where the work finds its form. You can't rush it. And you won't even begin to know the work, or the worth of it, until you finish your stay.

Camping, when you think about it, is work with an attitude of fun.

Pause: The Way Station

This isn't a destination, just a stopover. Here you take a breather from the wilderness. You clean up. Strip off the notions you've developed about your work, shedding your camp clothes, now oily with sweat and bug repellent and dusty with campfire smoke.

Lose attachments to your work. Step away. Stop judging. Find a way to disconnect so that when you return to your work, you can see with new eyes.

Once my husband and I walked into a restaurant after a weekend backpack trip, sweaty and disheveled. We wanted to tell the wait staff, "Hey! We really are better looking than this!" but there wasn't much we could say. We needed to brace ourselves for the stares we would get from the other patrons. Unfortunately, some writers set themselves up for insults and hurt feelings by not taking the time to stop and clean up.

Being in a hurry, many creators have left Draft Camp, brought their work to friends and associates—even fellow artists and writers, and received feedback that devastated them.

"But you don't understand!" they argued. In truth, these people hadn't spent enough time at the Way Station. They hadn't stripped off their attachments. Still wearing their camp clothes, they were thin-skinned about the whole thing.

And then there is another type of creator, who jumps from Draft Camp and heads for the road without stopping at the Way Station. As a writer, this person wants nothing to do with where he's been. He's ready for change, too ready. Old clothes? Burn them. Suggestions on improving the manuscript? Sure! Fire away! He'll take one and all suggestions, cutting out anything that might not work. He hasn't spent enough time away from the work to see the good in it.

He edits randomly, kamikaze. If not careful, this eager editor may cut away that which is valuable along with the dirt and grime. He has no idea what he's doing. He needs the Way Station.

For some, the Way Station is where they put their sketch or manuscript in a file and don't look at it for three months, one year, five years. The longer the time, the greater the distance. Over such a distance one can make better choices about where to go next.

The Way Station requires interminable patience. The scenery isn't great and you've got the feeling you're stuck, but you're not stuck.

Wait patiently so the answers can come to you. Don't be too demanding.

At this point, take careful thought of your route. Coming up next on the itinerary is Revision Village. You need to be prepared. Not only do you need distance, but sometimes you need a physical change to help you clear your Draft Camp mindset.

One writer physically moves her workspace. You can go to the kitchen table rather than write at your desk. Another writer takes his novel to the beach in solitude, pondering the whole of it. The Way Station calls for retreat.

It may mean giving yourself a pep talk so you aren't so attached to the work. It may mean preparing yourself to get feedback from others.

Visitors to the Way Station may read books, take a class or gather skills and knowledge to fuel the rest of their journey.

Sometimes, starting a new project is the best thing to do after reaching the Way Station. Put down your first project, leave it at the Way Station, go back to the Playground and see what develops. This way, when you are ready to pick up the first project, you'll know that your whole creative life doesn't consist of one tired old dog. You've got an adorable, brand new puppy needing your attention.

If you don't stop at the Way Station, chances are you won't be ready to face society. You may be the laughingstock of the town. You may strut around with a chip on your shoulder. You'll be dressed wrong. It may be difficult to stop when you're raring to go, but your work is worth it.

Some pitfalls: creators can get so enthralled with the fun of the playground and camping experience that they never want to leave. They dabble forever, adding this stroke of paint and that. Or they are in love with starting, and will start many projects, leaving them all at the Way Station. Unfortunately, they will never develop their skills until they take their projects completely through the Journey. Don't rush. But on the other hand, don't put off the Journey forever.

Station Three: Revision Village

I promised there'd be a chance to clean up and present yourself among society and here you are. In Revision Village, you gather input from other creators, and also from Dr. Codger. Yes, he is useful. (He can conduct himself just fine at parties if you keep the conversation steered to what he knows.) Assume your most cold, calculating Dr. Codger mode when you review your canvas or monologue, design or manuscript. Be ruthless about making changes.

Whatever your art form, find an objective way to assess quality. For writing, there are many good books on revising and editing that will give you a list of things to look for in Revision Village. Some great checklists include the famous *Elements of Style*, by Strunk and White. I like the straightforward sense of Stephen King's checklist in *On Writing*.

Most often, though, I hold my priorities subconsciously, depending on what I'm doing and what I'm interested in. Loosely, here are guidelines I draw upon for revision.

First, read the writing out loud. This is my number one tool. When you read aloud, a different part of your brain hears the work even though you may feel silly speaking to an empty room.

Your own voice holds power over your subconscious mind. You believe it. It affects you more deeply.

Besides reading alone, find a place where you can read your work for others. You'll be more sensitive to how the piece is coming across to your listeners, even without them saying a word. You may find yourself automatically shortening a sentence, substituting a word. Make note of your choices—your instincts are good.

Ask:

- How does the piece flow? How is the movement from one idea or scene to another? It might be gradual or snappy—as long as it has a sense of continuity and direction.

- Is the beginning a grabber? Is the first paragraph, image, or scene, one that compels the reader forward?

- Are there touchables? To interest the reader, you need details and objects which call the five senses into play. Are there colors, tastes, sounds, scents? Do you provide vivid images?

- Are you specific? Home in on one instance, moment or action, not the whole world. Don't let the writing be about everything and always, but about one object or action. Show the look on Aunt Marjorie's face. Give us the blue Nike dangling from the power line; let us hear the scream of the hawk.

- What is the ending note? The final paragraph or sentence should convey to your reader that this essay, article, poem or story has said what it needed to say. It may not give you the characters' future, or exhaust every last idea, yet the story feels complete.

Note where the reader loses interest. These are places you need to get to the point or bring action into a story. Perhaps you are not using enough concrete, riveting details. Maybe you sketched out the main points but didn't flesh in the fine points. Does your piece draw the reader in? Why or why not?

A writer may make several drafts of "telling" to find out what happens next. This is an important part of the process, but in the final revision needs to be cleared away or filled with juicy detail. Whole chapters or sections of books can run on incessantly providing few fresh scenes or ideas. Cut them, and don't be discouraged. To ease this loss, I save old drafts in a different document so that I can reuse deleted parts in the future. I rarely do, but I'm being kind to my Dream Kid.

Realize, even if you never use this material you are better for having spent creative time playing and camping.

Learn where your reader gets confused. Don't get in an argument with your reviewer and explain everything because you won't be there to do so for *all* your readers. Think about what your piece is saying, where it leaves the reader in the dark, and why.

Check for impact. Does this piece matter to the heart? Have you been honest about what was painful and challenging, whether in fiction or non-fiction? Notice where your reader laughs or sighs, becomes perfectly silent, shudders in fear, muses or says, "hmmm." Enjoy the emotional reactions. For this, we share our work.

More questions to ask:
- Where have you repeated yourself?
- What concepts or sentences need to be moved around?
- What can this piece do without?
- What scenes don't evoke the response you had hoped? Can they be moved? Can your story do without them?
- What paragraphs or sentences are out of place? Where might they better fit?
- What paragraphs or sentences can be cut? What about extra words?

When it comes to cutting words, there are a few simple markers. First of all, many possessive nouns such as mine, her, his, their, and our, can be cut. Just about anything you've said twice can be cut. In the previous sentence, "you've" can go away without changing meaning.

Adverbs, *mostly* can be deleted. As Mark Twain supposedly said, "If you see an adverb, kill it." But I need that "mostly" in the first sentence—because it says what I want to say.

Adjectives, too, are often unnecessary. Once again, this is dependent on a writer's style. If you love description, you will feature these words more than a minimalist writer would.

If you're not sure about a word, take it out. Put it back. Ah, this is the primary exercise of Revision Village.

As far as using the active or passive voice, there are some things to keep in mind. Take a look at these sentences:

a) Many books will tell you not to use passive sentences.

b) It is said in many books that passive sentences should not be used.

Passive sentences are usually long and clunky, as in sentence "b" above. You lose word weight and gain snap when you use active sentences such as sentence "a".

But bear in mind that for some kinds of writing, a passive voice diffuses emotional energy in a way that is necessary. For technical or legal papers this is true. A therapist writes patient notes using the passive voice, so as to focus on the patient's state, not on who did a particular action. Sometimes in writing we want to create that distance, whether through the dialogue of a shy aunt or a poem affecting a formal mood.

Another thing you'll want to look at is word choice. Notice which words stand out, and decide if you like the impression they create. Choose specific, sensory words over vague words wherever you can. Consider replacing weak words with strong, but always keep the tone in mind.

A note about strong words. Verbs like "wield" and "perambulate" are interesting choices, and they whisk the reader along. If I use "handle" or "walk" instead, the piece is quieter, more commonplace.

It all depends what sound the writer is going for. Muscular words were always my favorites until I began to see the value of quiet words, thanks to my astute teachers Joanna Rose and Stevan Allred of the Pinewood Table workshops. In fiction, the writer may wish to draw more attention to the story using spare and simple verbs. "Was" and "is" are good choices, although our high school English teachers shunned them. It's a matter of style, purpose and preference.

Revision Village is your place to look at your language and decide what it is doing. So often the answer is: "I don't know!" and then, it's patience, patience, patience. Back to the Way Station, back to reading, back to finding others who can provide feedback and help you see what the piece needs or doesn't.

Station Four: Publisher's Palace

It's where our dreams take us: autographing a book or giving a talk or displaying art at a gallery. We long to share what we've created with others. At the same time, the idea of being published is scary, and fraught with contradictory feelings. Some people have said, "I don't want to even go there," or "It's too hard to get published," or "I only create for myself." When I ask these people questions, more than anything else the responses sound like fear. Plain old fear, wrapped in a thousand guises.

Some of the thoughts behind the fears:

I'll never hit it big the way I've dreamed.

If I give my all and fail I'll look like a failure to everyone.

I'm afraid of what my friends and family will think, say or do.

My life will change and I'm not ready.

The one thing all these fears have in common is that you are the center of them.

Here's a little known fact about getting published: *It's not about you.*

The final stage of creation is sharing your gift with the world. It's not self-expression or earning accolades or finding the approval you didn't receive as a child. You have created and crafted a gift for the world. Now give it.

When you look at your creation this way, everything changes. Publishing becomes an opportunity. It's not a place for desperation.

Laura Stanfill, my friend and writing hero, is a fellow Pinewood Table participant. She has written three gorgeous novels which have caught the interest of editors and agents, yet after years of hard work (while at the same time raising two babies), she is an unpublished novelist. Has this stopped her? Not in the least. Laura is a successful blogger, editor, community leader and publisher in her own right. Recently she published an anthology of Oregon writers that serves to unite and inspire: *Brave on the Page: Oregon Writers on the Craft and the Creative Life.*

She points out that writing is brave, no matter how you look at it. "No matter what the cost, no matter what the outcome, we set our other obligations aside to write. And that's something to celebrate."

As owner of Forest Avenue Press, she plans to discover local novelists and bring their work to light. Laura gets it, that success is about focusing on what you can give, not on what you can get.

The truth is, success and failure don't loom in a stark dichotomy. When you understand that publishing is sharing, you will look for the people who need your gift instead of seeking how you can appear important. You will find someone who needs your uplifting words or funny comics or dark poetry. Someone out there will *feel* the work the way you do. They will know they're not alone when they see your art or read your story. It will make them happy, just as it has made you happy.

Again, here's the twist. Withholding your gift is selfishness. Fear is always selfish. When you're struggling to put yourself out there, think about what it is to hold back a great gift. Think of all the art and music and writing you've enjoyed in your own life because someone dared to give.

Find the people with whom your gift resonates. This search is worth your time.

Mostly, when people think or talk publication, they consider the big name publishers. It's much the same way the word "television" still evokes network television, while there are thousands of cable channels in existence. In today's world, the avenues provided by the Internet, grassroots movements, and your own community, are myriad. Again, publishing is not what you think.

Take your work to an open mike night at a coffee shop. Include a poem with a Christmas card. *Make* that Christmas card by hand. Start a blog. Self-publish a broadside at your local print shop. Ask the ice cream shop owner down the street if you can display your art. Turn your book into an e-book.

Publisher's Palace is the place for excruciatingly polished work. Give the best that you have in its finest form. Aim to thrill, terrify, amaze, entertain, educate, enlighten and grace other human beings. Stand tall on the ramparts of Publisher's Palace, where colorful banners whip in the wind and trumpets play.

Congratulations: you've completed your journey. Now get back there to Station One and start again.

The Creative Journey can be used for writing, creating, redecorating your bedroom or teaching your kid to drive. Trust it and be patient. Also don't be surprised if you need to revisit the Playground halfway through Draft Camp, or pause at Revision Village and backtrack to the Way Station, or move through Draft Camp multiple times. It's not a linear thing. If you backtrack without obsessing, bravo! You're getting it. The important thing is to begin with the Playground, creating with Dream Kid in charge.

You'll find your own rhythm and pattern, at times moving so swiftly that you won't consciously notice the shift of command from Dream Kid to Dr. Codger. *Yet you must always respect it.*

Each station has different priorities, and you need to be in the right mode for your station. Especially when you're frustrated or struggling, be sure you've got Dr. Codger in his place, and are allowing Dream Kid hers.

Spark 1

Consider a project you've completed. Can you recognize the stages you went through? Playground? Draft Camp? The Way Station? Revision Village? Publisher's Palace? Write a sentence or two summarizing what you did at each station.

Spark 2

Which station is the easiest for you? Which is the hardest? What do you avoid, and why? Do a ten minute wildwrite.

Spark 3

Make a map of the Creative Journey, showing the roadblocks you encounter at each station. Give your roadblocks or monsters or detours descriptive names (ala *Pilgrim's Progress*) like "Procrastinator's Peak" or the "Giants of What If," or "Excuse Alley."

Spark 4

Do you allow yourself to play? Where? What do you stick with? When do you camp out? Where do you refine? What do you bring to completion, giving your best? Journal about this.

CHAPTER TWENTY

Authenticity

"Give me the man of honest heart, I care not what he be;
he may be rich, he may be poor, it matters not to me."

—from "Give Me the Man of Honest Heart," a song by C. Stedman

ONE OF my Wildfire Writers, Jeff, describes an interesting problem.

There is a personality that I keep hidden inside and never let out. Two reasons for this secrecy come to mind. The first is that the secret personality is precious. It is who I believe myself to be. It is something that if taken away from me, would make me feel as if I had died—or would make me wish I had. The second has to do with the vulnerability of that personality. It is somewhat defenseless. It is quite easily hurt.

These two issues, coupled together have resulted in my adapting a strategy of secrecy. Perhaps that sounds overly dramatic, but it has been my experience from childhood. The defense against hurt was to make what I value invisible. There are several strategies for this, including camouflage and obfuscation. Keeping the personality quiet and withdrawn is also part of the process of keeping it safe.

So I am wondering. Does the inner personality die stillborn within me? Or at some point, is he to be allowed out, to exercise his particular brand of creativity? How is this to be done?

I've come across many creative people like Jeff who have learned to protect one self within, an imaginative, rich, creative personality, while projecting another self in the day-to-day world where money is made and responsibilities are met.

There is something to be said about having a persona that can assist you in certain areas. The challenge is, though, that many creative people don't fully experience who they are. To me, this is one of the dangers of social networking: I'm afraid if I spend too much time at it, I might start to believe in my online role more than my true self.

If you are constantly playing a role, you limit your impact. The person you were created to be is underground. When you daily reject your inner inclinations and doubt yourself, you deep-freeze your true passions.

The fire won't roar when it's artificial. If you've been trained to spend all your time playing a role that isn't really you, not much action will happen when you strike the match.

Many of us have been judged in regard to what we thought or felt. Perhaps you were pressured, as I was, to play the part of the "well-adjusted" child. We weren't allowed to feel what we really felt, and most definitely not allowed to show it.

Maybe you spent years training yourself to seem okay when you weren't. You pretended to be happy if you were sad; a rock fan if you loved country music; a vegetarian if you craved meat. Over time, you almost convinced yourself that you were somebody else.

One of my own coping strategies has been to appear outgoing and happy. This meant taking on more and more extroverted obligations. In my work as a writing coach, I began suffering burnout because I was focusing on teaching several large classes every week. I was managing many group gatherings and social elements. Since solitude is where I'm renewed, it's no surprise that I ran out of energy.

When it struck me what was going on, I was afraid to change.

My fears:

- *How will I survive financially?*
- *What if people stop liking me?*
- *What if I become a hermit?*
- *What if I lose clients or students?*

Yet a voice kept telling me, "Take the risks." The message would come out in my journal, again and again. I had to be myself, or I would grow to hate the work.

When I changed my schedule to revolve around solitary workdays, I was more than okay. New clients came my way, and I had more energy for people in evenings and weekends. I didn't become a hermit. I experienced a surge of creativity and productivity. For the first time in a long while, I didn't feel the need to fight my own nature.

To start recognizing the secret self, express it. Bellow, boast, whine, or howl. I've put together the following ideas to help you come out of hiding.

Throwaway Book

Write or draw what you feel in a notebook, sketchbook, or on scraps of paper—then toss it. There are no rules about how or when to dispose of the pages. You might even decide to save it, but you'll take on a devil-may-care attitude.

I think of all the journals I left blank over the years, before giving myself permission to use them. Dr. Codger would watch over my shoulder as I attempted the first line. *"That's dumb! You call that poetry?* Or, *How can you say that about your mother?"* Writing and drawing messy, throwaway work taught me to turn off his voice.

A throwaway journal frees you. You and Dr. Codger cut a deal. "Listen," you tell him. "I get to write whatever I want. This is only junk, worthy of throwing away."

You relax and ignore scribbles and messes, ink smears and distorted drawings. Punctuation, grammar, spelling and horrendous handwriting don't interrupt your flow.

Spark 1

Paste torn-out journal entries on a poster board. Paint, watercolor or draw over them in any style that suits your mood. Save or discard your art.

Spark 2

Make cuttings of your pages—from snowflakes to spirals. Use scrapbooking scissors for unusual shapes.

Spark 3

Take your journal to the beach. Dig a hole in the sand and light a small fire. Once the pages are ashes, watch the waves wash them away.

Protecting Your Fire

Along with freedom to create from your secret self, you also need practical wisdom. Make sure no one has access to your writing but you. There was a time when my journals were being read, and I naively continued to leave them in the open. Each time the intruder read my words, I was wounded. Guard yourself against this possibility.

Surround yourself with people you can trust, but consider a lockbox, computer password, or hiding place for your work. Let others know they must respect your privacy. This is your right.

Shattering Taboos

We all have thoughts we'd never say out loud. Curses, terrors, protests, stupid questions. They become taboo. Some of these stem from family backgrounds, while others are personal. You won't see them until you are willing to do so.

Once you identify your taboos, voicing them can be a peaceful rebellion. Writing or drawing a taboo can be a source of real power and fire.

Growing up with foster parents who were ministers, I wanted more than anything to fit in. I rarely questioned anything I was taught about faith and church: in my mind, doubts were taboo. When I gained courage as an adult to explore these taboos on paper, my faith took on a shape that fit me exactly.

Spark 1

Write for fifteen minutes about a taboo you have never allowed yourself to speak about. Afterward feel free to destroy your writing.

Spark 2

Reflect on the taboo in the previous spark. Call your taboo the name of an animal, any animal. A gray, lone wolf. A menacing weasel. A poisonous ant. Draw this animal, as big and boldly as you can. Perhaps it is a made up-beast. Describe the shape and color and smell of it. Don't mention any of the words associated with the taboo, just describe the animal.

CHAPTER TWENTY-ONE

Fake It 'til You Make It

"There was a time when you fooled ev'ryone
and you fooled me too."

—from "Who Did You Fool After All?" a song by Van & Schenck and Johnny S. Black

NOW THAT WE'VE LAUDED the joys of authenticity, let's indulge fakery. Just as lying can boost your creativity, acting can be a great tool for your creative tool box.

Most of us act in many ways, all the time. We have an act for the workplace and especially for the job interview. We have an act for Grandma's house and for opening gifts at Christmas. And there is an act we use at church, or with our neighbors, or when we make a public presentation.

When I was in junior high school, my sweet foster mom would say, "Why do you act like Pollyanna around your friends? It's okay to be yourself, you know." My shiny, happy face was a facade I thought I needed in order to be liked. I had developed that persona to help me survive my childhood, and I didn't even realize it.

As an adult, I hated the thought that I still might be using my act. I became distrustful of myself whenever I caught myself putting on a persona.

Through the years, every time I went into Pollyanna mode, a voice deep down would remind me to be more genuine. Over time, I worked on being that genuine self, and I still do. And yet I came to understand that this persona was a valuable help. It allowed me to do the following:

- attend a conference
- write a cover letter
- teach a class
- submit a bio
- make a proposal
- publish a website
- write a press release
- keep a blog
- introduce myself

My friend, the author and poet Sage Cohen, is an excellent publicist for her own work. She is quick to send out bold press releases, blurbs, and announcements of her many achievements, and yet she is a warm and un-assuming person, as genuine as they come. When I told her how much I admired her abilities as a self-promoter, she confided her secret: "I pretend I'm talking about someone else."

Sage didn't need to identify too closely with that author, poet and teacher. She could remove herself to a comfortable distance and operate from creative pretending. The persona helped her to achieve more than she otherwise could have.

Regardless of my roles and personas, the important thing is that I stay connected to the true me. It's like they tell you in show business: "Never believe your own press." You can't start treating your personas as if they are more real than the deep-down you. I make best use of my "pretending"—or fakery, if you will, while staying in touch with myself. Some ways I remember who I am: daily journaling, meditation, friendship, walking, and solitude. In the middle of the day, I'll check in: "What am I feeling right now?"

I can conserve the most creative me—hidden and shadowed, deep and emotional—while allowing the persona to promote my work, stay upbeat, and network with others. At the end of performing these roles, I can objectively ask, "How did the marketer do today?" or "What does the public relations manager need this week?" These roles are not me. I don't have to take them personally or obsess over them.

At the same time, I invite true, authentic elements into my persona. Today I'm wearing a rhinestone roadrunner pin that belonged to my grandmother. I illustrate lectures by drawing cartoons on the white board. I start classes with a crazy check-in question. These bits of who I am shine through my roles.

In the book *Success without a College Degree*, John T. Murphy writes, "If you're not completely satisfied with who you are, create a character . . . ." This person then acts the way you *wish* you could.

Your imagination is much more than a tool for drawing pictures or writing stories. Use it to color your presence in the world.

If you do create a character for yourself, be sure it aligns with who you were *meant* to be. Then by all means, start acting like that person—all the time. At first it will feel like acting; Dr. Codger will insist you're a fraud and tell you to knock it off. Here's where the "'til you make it" part comes in. When you go beyond the protestations of Dr. Codger, you'll find this person you are reaching for was real all along—part of the greater, hidden you.

Who knows? I might have a little Pollyanna in my soul.

Spark 1

Explore these questions by drawing a picture or writing a page.

- *When have you successfully used a persona?*
- *When have you felt like a phony? Did you ever quit a role that helped you do some things?*
- *When have you gotten your role mixed up with the real you?*

CHAPTER TWENTY-TWO

The Taming of the Groke

"My heart was frozen, even as the earth."

—from "A Spirit Flower," a song by Martin Stanton

IN TOVE JANSSON'S classic book *Moominland Midwinter*, the Groke is a forlorn, frightening creature whose frosty touch kills everything in her path. Longing for warmth, she unwittingly breaks up parties, ruins picnics, and sends people packing. She cannot help being who she is, a shapeless monster. All she wants is company.

Every creative person has a frozen Groke lurking at the edge of camp, hungry for creativity but unable to generate anything. The Groke can easily destroy passion. She is another face of Dr. Codger, running amok and misunderstood. Sadly, she may take the form of a teacher, friend, or relative.

Reflect on your own encounters with the Groke.

Spark 1

When was the first time the Groke put out your fire for an idea, work of art, or project? What was said? How did you react? Recreate the scene.

Spark 2

Does your Groke have a face or first name? When is your Groke most active? How does your Groke attack? What words does she use to douse the flames of your creativity? When are you most susceptible to her ice? Draw a comic of your Groke, demonstrating these points, complete with a conversation bubble.

Why You Need the Groke

If allowed too close, too soon, the Groke will smother any fire you start. But it's a complicated problem. We require the merest hint of her presence in order to succeed.

We creators can burn so high that we don't see our work for what it is. We need objectivity.

Out of all the Wildfire Writers I've encountered, ninety-five percent talked about loving their newfound freedom. Finally they could say, imagine, and create anything at all. But gradually I became aware of another kind of writer, though rare. Five percent came to class having written volumes of work with absolutely no critical interference from Dr. Codger. Disappointingly, their writing put most of the class to sleep. These writers made it a point not to revise their work, and they never improved. Their writing was strung-together words that went on for hundreds of pages but could not teach them the writing process. There wasn't much by way of story. I was puzzled by these writers, who had terrific ideas and were talented human beings. Then I realized the problem. The Groke was too far from the picture.

These writers needed a little threat, needed to wake up to the cold and discover there was work to be done. They didn't need frostbite or anything, just a little exposure.

Our fires can make us comfortable and lazy when there is still much to do. It's crucial that we hone our work, reworking and revising. We can't simply move away from the Groke: we have to work *with* her.

Once our fire is well underway, we need to accept the Groke at a safe distance. Her cooling blasts help us move through the process, showing us specific areas of weakness. When a writer fills page after page in a burst of energy, he may find himself petering out with the vague sense that something is not right. If he refuses to acknowledge any flaws or problems, in time he will quit.

He must turn and face the Groke.

Let the Groke help you with an honest assessment of your project, once you are strong enough.

Spark

Consider a specific project. Are you ready for the Groke? Wildwrite about how you will strike a careful balance with the Groke. What is the Groke saying that might help you? How can you use her information?

CHAPTER TWENTY-THREE

The Incineration of Procrastination

"Never put off till tomorrow what may be done
day after tomorrow just as well."

—Mark Twain

ARE YOU ORGANIZING a desk drawer, updating your computer, or sorting paintbrushes instead of working on the thing you should be working on? Welcome to the finger-drumming, toe-tapping, stalled-out world of procrastination.

You can't overcome procrastination by daydreaming. You can't fix it by ignoring it. Good intentions can't correct it. Sheer willpower can't break its steel grip. I have, however (grinning proudly), found an approach that works. Or maybe it just helps me feel better while I'm still procrastinating.

Here is the path:

1) Relax.

2) Call it.

3) Stop judging.

4) Seek the meaning.

5) Find something good.

6) Welcome the resistance.

7) Observe the consequences.

8) Determine what you need.

9) Connect with the bigger picture.

Let's take a closer look at these steps.

- *Relax.* Remember that a creative journey begins in the Playground. Maybe you're pressing too hard. Breathe.

- *Call it.* If you're procrastinating, be honest and admit it. You can't deal with the problem if you're pretending it's not there.

- *Stop judging.* If you never complete your task, at least you can stop taking yourself so seriously.

- *Seek the meaning* behind the resistance. In *Writing On Both Sides of the Brain,* Henriette Anne Klauser explains that whenever you feel resistance, there is always a message in it.

I have found many reasons for resistance, such as:

- The need for incubation. You might be dragging your heels because you need incubation time. Dream Kid requires stretches of undemanding time in order to formulate her thoughts.

- The discomfort of getting started. There is a sense of confusion that accompanies the beginning of a work of art or fiction.

- Failing. Maybe you are putting off working on a great article idea because you're worried it won't be very good.

- Emotional Pain. For a long time, getting to my autobiographical novel was high on my wish list but low on my action list. I was procrastinating because I didn't want to focus on several painful memories that were integral to the work.

- Missing Pieces. Perhaps you need more information or tools in order to complete the work. This could be as simple as needing stamps or a new sketchbook.

- Fear of Success. Maybe, deep down, you don't really want this project to succeed, because it might change your life in some way.

Identifying fears and rationale can be complicated; it takes time and self-honesty. But once you begin to see the meaning behind your procrastination, you're ready for the next step.

Find something good. Put a positive spin on your procrastination. Whether it's Dr. Codger nitpicking, or the Groke blasting you with icy hopelessness, you can reinterpret the procrastination in a positive light.

Maybe your lag time has helped ideas to germinate.

If you can't bring yourself to create, find something you *can* do. Anything counts. Research your topic or visit an art gallery or talk to an artist. Most of all, stop being hard on yourself.

What do I procrastinate doing? Making submissions. I have so many different kinds of writing that I get overwhelmed; it's the same way I feel when sorting a huge load of laundry. My brain doesn't like separating socks out of one basket into different directions. I used to get down on myself for this.

Now, I just remind myself that I'm an idea person. I may not empty the basket quickly, but I fill it with ease, collecting ideas by the load.

When Dr. Codger tells me I'm stupid or indecisive, I tell him I'm gifted, and it's easier for me to act.

When you give yourself credit, you gain new confidence. You'll feel relaxed, positive and ready to move forward. I cannot emphasize enough how important it is to create these positive emotions in your writing life—they make all the difference.

Welcome the resistance. Draw a picture or go for a walk and think gently about your resistance. This new outlook can take you from waging a war with yourself to feeling at peace.

Observe the consequences of your procrastination. What's the worst thing that may happen if you don't paint/create/sing/write? What is the worst price you've ever had to pay for procrastinating? On the other hand, what's the best thing that might happen if you take on the job? Visualize your success. See your completed play being performed or your song being sung. Imagine yourself autographing your book at a bookstore event.

Determine what you need to move forward. It's okay to have needs and limitations. Who wouldn't stall, needing tools, information, or a different approach? Sitting there listening to the ongoing negative litany of your writing enemies is one way to keep you from meeting your own needs.

For my novel, I needed patience and determination to work through emotional material. I let myself talk through difficult points with a counselor and explored them in my journal. Once the healing was underway, I wrote the entire manuscript and started a second book.

Connect with the bigger why that makes you create in the first place. Remind yourself of your hope, dream and talent.

With this kind of courage, you'll never get around to organizing your desk drawer or sorting your paintbrushes. You'll be swept up in the blaze of working toward your dreams.

Spark 1

Make a list of every creative idea you're procrastinating about. Now highlight one idea that speaks to you. Take some action on this idea, however small.

Spark 2

On a sheet of paper, draw a line down the center. On the left write the possible consequences of your procrastination. On the right, list the hoped-for outcomes of taking action. Assess on paper whether it's worth it to seize the day, or whether procrastinating has a bigger payoff.

CHAPTER TWENTY-FOUR

Creating Through a Crisis

Only a poet sorts *grief*—
a riptide shredding
bodies on rocks—from
mourning—bones
rolled by surf.

—from "What Poets Do," a poem by Kate Gray

SOMETIMES LIFE drags us through knotholes backwards. When I lost my birth mom to Parkinson's disease, grief made everything hard, especially writing. My husband and I were having financial struggles. And I had just learned my uncle had cancer.

"I'm too stressed to write," I told my friend.

"You have to take care of yourself," she said. But as I hung up the phone I was thinking of other people I knew who had stopped writing or doing photography or theatre because of events that taxed their emotions. In time, they were halted by new problems that came along. Eventually the sparks of their creativity faded away.

Wildfire Writing asks you to make a choice when the world is sad, stressful or confusing. It teaches that your creative power is ready to be drawn upon, regardless of how blank the page, how scattered your mind, or what is going on in your life. You may be experiencing emotional, financial or physical stress. Still, your creativity can survive.

When life overwhelms you, here are seven ways to take care of yourself.

Put yourself first

If you have suffered serious loss, death or divorce, there's nothing you can do but grieve. Give yourself a wide margin; let projects drop. Remember: the creative fire is burning within you, and everything that helps and heals the artist will promote the work.

At the same time, think about how your fire might warm you. Seek comfort in your art. Getting away with a notebook may supply a needed stress-break. Conjuring an off-the-wall short story or a prayerful poem may bring a moment of peace.

Journal your frustrations, indulge your sadness. Write letters. Use your creative talent every day, just for the satisfaction, without considering whether it's a "useful" project.

Do low-energy work

If you can, finish something you started a while back. Don't demand fresh material. Get out a half-blank canvas. Polish an old manuscript. Keep it easy.

After my birth mother died, I couldn't work under my own initiative. Taking a writing course provided steady assignments, stitching a straight row of writing seams into my crooked days. Rather than rely on yourself, find a coach, instructor or class to lower the amount of energy it takes to keep you writing.

Surprisingly, this is also your chance to write something you normally wouldn't. Psychologists say that in emotional crisis, aspects of creativity are heightened rather than diminished. Your energy is too depleted for Dr. Codger to care about criticizing your work. Dream Kid can play by herself. So go ahead and try something wild, just because. Keep it short. Submit an entry to a writing contest. Do some wordplay.

You can't give it all your attention right now, and that's okay.

Shrink expectations

The last thing you need is more pressure. Go easy on yourself, or as the saying goes, "Try softer."

Take your normal expectation and cut it. If formerly your quota was one painting a month, try half a painting a month.

Recognize that others around you don't have a barometer. They can only guess at what to expect. Instead of keeping up appearances that you can do it all, acknowledge that you need days off work, or time away from this committee, or help with that project.

Put your problem to work

Instead of making it the reason you *can't* create, see how your problem can work for you. Let it give you a reason for taking extra time.

With Mother's death, I didn't have the heart to rub shoulders in social circles. I explained to family that journaling helped me in my grieving process. With fewer obligations, I began writing more.

Go ahead and pare down your responsibilities by telling people about your life. "My dad's sick," or "I'm starting a new job," or "My wife's going in for a biopsy." Whatever your situation, use it to purchase creating time. With the aid of others, you can carve out corners for taking care of yourself through creativity.

Stomp out your stress

Physical exercise can help alleviate emotional and mental pressure. One writer I know spent years at her daily writing regimen while she grew depressed and her body slowly declined. At a doctor's advice, she left off the writing and incorporated morning walks into her routine. Her mental outlook improved, and so did her health and her writing. Consider a swim, game of tennis, bike ride—whatever you can incorporate into your life.

Engineer creativity benefits into your activity. For example, I love to bounce thoughts off a walking partner: I'm getting exercise and ideas at the same time. I've had some inspiring, art-centered conversations while walking with theatre directors, photographers, healers, potters and art therapists. Before busting your butt on the treadmill, grab a magazine that will further knowledge in your field. Make the library, art supply store or bookstore a walking destination.

Write in shorter bursts

When busy or upset, you won't be able to spend hours at your work. Being consistent is more important than generating volumes. Set a timer for ten minutes after dinner and delegate the dishes. Skip the evening news and go write or create. Make these little bits a priority, keeping your creative work alive. When tempted to give them up, ask people around you for help. Carry a notebook and pull it out when waiting in line, stuck in traffic, or on hold with someone on the phone.

Make necessary repairs

Don't keep on paddling if your ship is sinking. If you're having a crisis, especially a middle-sized one that doesn't take your full attention, you might put it out of your mind, escaping to your studio or desk. We creative people can focus, and stoke those flames, and that's good. But sometimes you and I need to tackle problems head-on.

This may be true when a family member needs you, when you're ignoring a health problem, or when you're wishing away a financial crisis. Stop your routine and patch the boat—so you can get back to creating.

When I was grieving Mother and our money problems hit, I couldn't seem to act. Finally I saw that counting on my normal work to make up for financial losses was a mistake at this time.

I signed with a temporary agency and used my secretarial skills to take things one at a time, making a steady paycheck. Financial pressures lifted until I could get back into my routine.

What temporary, practical measures can you take to relieve stress? It may be getting a part-time job, hiring a babysitter, taking a retreat at the beach to focus on your art. The important thing to recognize is that your stressful time won't last forever. Whatever you do to care for yourself will fuel your creative flame.

Spark

Copy the following creed and keep it on your dashboard. Say it out loud at stoplights.

Stressed Creator's Creed

I can't do everything perfectly, and that's okay.

I don't have to produce great stuff right now.

I have all the time I need to finish my (novel, oil painting, screenplay, etc).

I can always reach out for help.

Other creators have succeeded in the face of this, and I can too.

I'm valuable and talented.

I'm committed to my art.

I'll get through this and keep on creating.

CHAPTER TWENTY-FIVE

Beware the Creeper

"An ambition is a little creeper that creeps and creeps in your heart night and day, singing, 'Come and find me, come and find me.'"

—Carl Sandburg, *Rootabaga Stories*

IT'S POSSIBLE to get stuck on the idea of being an artist or writer. Life can pass you by while you're wishing for people to notice your work. This hunger is never appeased. In his fanciful *Rootabaga Stories,* Carl Sandburg tells of three boys who lived in the Village of Liver-and-Onions:

"So here we have 'em, three boys growing up with wishes, suspicions, and mixed up wishes and suspicions." They shared a secret ambition which "crept into their hearts and made them sad, too sad, so sad it was hard to live."

I love the whimsical way Sandburg has described this feeling. Ambition can become a strangling force, crying, "I can't be happy unless this happens!" You and I make all kinds of rules about what we need in order to be happy. Writing becomes a duty that saps energy.

Who you are is far more important than anything you could ever achieve. Dr. Codger can't fathom this. He has pushed our society into making everyone think they *are* their work. Notice at the next party you attend, how introductions put emphasis on work, roles and titles.

If your sense of worth is dependent on your career, your well-being will always be fragile and precarious. Those folks who insist on getting noticed and published and recognized are never satisfied, because there is always more "out there." There is always another juried show, another award or review, just out of reach. And so the happiness one expected vanishes like a mirage on a desert horizon.

Your creativity is a way to honor yourself rather than become enslaved. You have already arrived.

Always put your emphasis on who you are. That secret spirit, invisible to the world, created in unconditional love. If you do not know this person, start by accepting him or her. Be willing to spend time just being—without judging, evaluating or condemning.

Writing, creating, composing, painting—these things then become a by-product of you being you.

Your Dream Kid thrives in an atmosphere of acceptance and rest rather than striving and desperation. *If you are desperate to succeed, you've already missed the point of your life.*

Spark 1

Write a love letter to yourself, describing the wonderful essence that is you, without making reference to any titles you have, roles you play, or things you've achieved.

Spark 2

Make a list of all the benefits your creativity brings you, regardless of results and outcomes.

CHAPTER TWENTy-SIX

The Art of Inkling

Barn

Throw your shoulder
into the weight
of door lay down
your human
condition roll in
the sweet hay
of horse secrets
feast
on the nothing
you know

by Sage Cohen

THE CREATIVE PROCESS happens along the border of an unknown country. This unexplored place is what scares and exhilarates a creator. As Greg says, "My novel has a great beginning. But after chapter four, I haven't got a clue what happens."

Mary says, "I have no idea how to write my memoir conclusion."

Val says, "I'm not sure what I'm doing, but I'm interested in trying a new voice." The unknown is always there, always a bit uncomfortable. We can either fight it, or learn to accept it as a fact of the writing life.

110

The old saying "write what you know" may be more about emotional truth than physical truth, or else, how could fantasy writers, mythmakers, and historical novelists do their work? We set ourselves up for a struggle when we insist on knowing everything. If you stay with what you know, there will be no growth or adventure. The closer you get to the unknown hinterlands, the more creative and interesting and unique your work will be.

Those who insist on sticking with one thing will be rigid and closed to new possibilities when they come along. This isn't to say you can't plan or work from an outline. Sketches and plans are wonderful tools. But when they become the only way, wonder and mystery disappear.

Even detailed outliners make multitudes of changes. This book went through four title changes before I'd written a hundred pages. For all that time, I didn't know what half the chapters would be about. But I did have an inkling. And this is what you do with the unknown: you inkle.

To inkle is to let your unknowing be. Have you ever seen a lake covered with morning mist? Wisps of steam float upon the surface, obscuring the water. You know that later, as the sun rises, the mist will dissipate and you'll see the lake beneath.

Have you ever seen anyone stomp out on such a lakeshore and try to push the mist away? Perhaps with a leaf blower. This is what we look like to the universe when we insist on knowing every little thing.

Much of the beauty of life, and of creating, lies in the unseen and unknown.

Here's another way to inkle. You're driving through a tunnel at night, with just enough light to see the concrete walls, but you can't see the exit. Do you panic? Do you fear that there is no exit? Just because you don't see it doesn't mean it isn't there. You inkle, expecting that the tunnel will soon end, and you drive on calmly.

People inkle in all sorts of situations. But when we are uneasy, we want more information. We become frustrated when we don't know what happens in a story we are writing, or when we don't know how to balance the contours in a sculpture we have begun. These unknowns are discovered through the process. Inkling consists of one part trust, one part hopeful expectation, and five parts patience. It's a vital part of creative living.

Spark 1

Get in the car and head in any direction for one hour. Stop at a rest stop or coffee shop or grocery store, and write or sketch the landscape and the people walking by. Maybe you'll end up at Joe's Gas Station next to a beat-up green Plymouth carrying two cats, a dog, and a gentleman with a handlebar mustache. Or maybe you'll end up on Main Street in front of a crumbling brick building. Find out what you don't know about the place where you didn't know you were going.

Spark 2

Consider a problem in your life that you can't see the end of. It may be a financial problem, a health problem, a personality conflict with a friend or co-worker. Close your eyes. Tell yourself: *I'll find my way through this.* Imagine driving through a foggy tunnel at night.

Breathe deeply.

Now inkle.

Finish this sentence: *I know that someday I'll understand about . . . .*

CHAPTER TWENTY-SEVEN

What You Know

"Of course I know them all, dear,
it's nothing strange you see."

—from "It's My Business to Know Them All," a song by Joe Goodwin

MOST OF US DON'T KNOW what we know. We ignore it in search of new knowledge. The cool thing about embracing the ordinary facts of your life is that you begin to appreciate all that you already know. It's helpful to incorporate this knowledge in bits and pieces, or as inspiration for a major work. A midwife may choose to write about home birth. A traveler may paint a skyline of a city she has visited. A tortured adolescent may grow up to create comedy sketches for young adults.

Taking a look at all that you know is essential for contributing to others' knowledge. As the saying goes, if you want to learn something, teach it. If you make your knowledge available to others, then you'll understand it even more profoundly. For this reason, exploring your memories can be helpful. Look at every experience of your life, and consider ways you could embellish these experiences or amplify or beautify them. How can your life lessons help someone else? See your experiences through eyes that have *never* experienced them. They're nothing to take for granted.

A writer in my class who despaired of having any original ideas was challenged to "write about color as if describing it to a blind person." Lo and behold, Lance found out he knew more about color than he thought he did. He learned that his gift for physical seeing was related to the original way that he looked at the world. He wrote pages and pages of amazing color poems, publishing a rainbow-hued chapbook.

This came about because Lance was willing to work with what he knew and not assume that everyone else knew it, too. (*Yeah, it's just the color red. So what?*)

Spark 1

Make a list of facts about yourself, such as:

- birthplace
- birth marks or physical details
- physical capabilities (My daughter can make camel lips. My stepson can dance like a character in a Peanut's cartoon)
- once-in-a-lifetime experiences
- food attractions and revulsions
- places you've been
- celebrities you've met
- unique family stories—how your grandparents met, what your great uncle did for a living
- quirky co-workers
- conversations you've had on a bus or plane
- strange coincidences
- quirky traits (I use a pillow for ten minutes every night, then throw it on the floor. My sister eats mashed potatoes with corn on top)
- observations you've made about life
- weird neighbors you've known

- experiments you've made that worked or failed miserably
- practical jokes you've suffered or played on someone else
- areas of professional expertise
- people you are an expert at dealing with
- your home town and its inhabitants

Spark 2

List ten major life experiences.

Ask:

for someone who hasn't gone through this (or gone through it yet), what do I know that I can teach? Through my art form, how can I reinterpret the experience, giving someone a new perspective?

CHAPTER TWENTY-EIGHT

Slow Down

"Why should we be in such desperate haste to succeed, and
in such desperate enterprises?"

—Henry David Thoreau, *Walden*

YOU CAN'T CREATE a masterpiece at breakneck speed. Though it's not popular, easy, or productive at first glance, creativity requires slowing down and
incubating. Guy Claxton, in *Hare Brain, Tortoise Mind: How Intelligence
Increases When You Think Less,* presents studies showing the brain's capac-
ity for different kinds of processing. "Some of its functions," he writes, "are
performed at lightning speed; others take seconds, minutes, hours, days or
even years to complete their course." Claxton argues that the slower ways
of thinking are often the highest, most creative, and most productive over
the long haul.

He describes our modern problem. "The slow ways of knowing will not
deliver their delicate produce when the mind is in a hurry. In a state of con-
tinual urgency and harassment, the brain-mind's activity is condemned to
follow its familiar channels. Only when it is meandering can it spread and
puddle . . . ."

Author Brenda Ueland refers to this puddling as "moodling." It is her
word for "long inefficient, happy idling, dawdling and puttering." In 1938,
decades before modern brain research, Ueland wrote that moodling is

necessary for the writer, because "inspiration comes very slowly and quietly." (*If You Want to Write*) Ueland continues:

> *That is why I hope you can keep up this continuity and sit for some time every day (if only for a half hour, though two hours is better and five is remarkable and eight is bliss and transfiguration!) before your typewriter, —if not writing then just thoughtfully pulling your hair. If you skip for a day or two, it is hard to get started again. In a queer way you are afraid of it. It takes again an hour or two of vacant moodling, when nothing at all comes out on paper; and this is difficult always because it makes us . . . with our accomplishment-mania, feel uneasy and guilty.*

Ah, yes. She has hit the nail on the head, perhaps even more perfectly in the 2010's than in the 1930's. Slowing down and taking time for quiet, thoughtful activity makes us feel guilty because we're taught it's useless. Once again, Dr. Codger is imposing his relentless rules. He'd rather we look busy, and accomplish nothing, than appear lazy even when growing the seed of a masterpiece idea.

We creators have to buck up, to defy Dr. Codger and be different. We must take time out, turning off the "harassments" of modern technology. I recommend setting aside uninterrupted time every week. This could be one to three hours. We should also set aside an entire creativity weekend every three to six months.

People argue with me that such a break is impossible. They don't have time to "do nothing," even for an hour. They say, "My kids need me," or "I've got to make a living," or "I can't afford time off." And though they might be writers and musicians and artists, they create only in their sparest spare time after every other conceivable chore and responsibility has been completed. In other words, they put themselves last. Even if they do beg, borrow, or steal some time, they're so frazzled they don't have the mental acuity or soulful resources needed for creating. Here's what I've noticed about these folks. Many have health problems while others are irritable and bitter. Their marriages are strained. They're teaching their kids to put themselves last, too.

All are running, as if from someone or something.

Today's pace isn't just about time. It's about mental space. Distractions, information feeds, and the adrenaline rush of multi-tasking choke our chance to experience the moment. Technology offers instant news, entertainment and preoccupation. Our iPods are churning out noise, our fingers are itching for smart phones and keyboards, and our eyes are being lured by the megapixeled colors of digital screens. Art, by contrast, is created and experienced in the moment.

At first, turning off the gadgets makes life seem boring. Yet this is a phase we must pass through in order to get our minds and time back. I, too, struggle with this modern problem. Working on this chapter, I paused to make a Facebook post, and then learned it was an old friend's birthday, and just had to check photos of her party, and before I knew it I'd clicked on a dozen people and events. Even though I was at the computer for my designated hour, it didn't seem long enough. An hour of work, broken up by Twitter or email or cell phone messages, can feel like twenty minutes. By contrast, when I write at our family cabin, where there's no Internet access, I experience a slowing down. An hour without distractions expands to feel significant and valuable, part of a good day's work.

This slowing down isn't an actual measuring of time density: the seconds in each minute or the minutes in each hour. It's an awareness of how pace affects mind, soul, body. All this impacts creativity.

I dare you to try it. Minimize distractions. For part of your day, do one thing at a time.

Some people won't get it, thinking you're a mastodon. Are you willing to be misunderstood? Can you retrain your "accomplishment-mania?" Will you find a creative way to meet your budget instead of using every spare minute to make money? Can you settle down your click-happy fingers and your hyperactive brain? Many generations incorporated a Sabbath or rest day as a sacred practice. Heck, thirty years ago, markets, shops and gas stations were closed on Sundays. Today it's up to you to commit to this discipline.

Not only will you boost your creativity, but you'll reduce stress, cultivate health, improve your relationships, sharpen your intellect and ease your soul.

Spark 1

Brain Rest. Sit comfortably in a quiet place. Breathe deeply, noticing how the breath feels as it flows in and out of your body. When thoughts come, imagine them lifting like soap bubbles and floating away. Continue letting the soap bubbles float away as you breathe, sit, and rest for ten minutes.

Spark 2

Longhand. Copy a passage from a beloved book. It slows you down and transmits wisdom and beauty in a visceral way. Some of my favorite choices include *Walden* by Thoreau, a Psalm from the Bible, any poem by William Stafford, or *Pilgrim at Tinker Creek*, by Annie Dillard. Write a sentence or paragraph (in cursive if possible, but print is acceptable), paying attention to the flow of letters. Critical thoughts may come about your handwriting or the crookedness of your lines; dismiss them. Experience the flow of words from pen into fingers, along your arm, into your spine.

CHAPTER TWENTY-NINE

Speed Up

"In skating over thin ice our safety is in our speed."

—Ralph Waldo Emerson, "Prudence," Essays, First Series

SPEED can be a great ally. It allows Dream Kid to come to the fore, causing Dr. Codger to lag behind. Here are some creative activities best done quickly.

- Brainstorming. Let those ideas fast-fire, whether with a group or on your own.
- Wildwriting. For a specific amount of time, with a timer to stop you, write as fast as you can. The faster you go, the sooner you outrace the critic.
- Movement. Research is uncovering that moving fast is good for you. Depressed patients have shown improvement through "speed therapy" carrying out everyday movements at a faster pace. Similarly, aerobic exercise provides a charge of happy hormones for health and well-being. What "fast activity" can you incorporate into your week?
- Doing something you fear. Instead of giving yourself time to think about it, hurry forward before your mind talks you out of it. Whenever I'm invited to speak or give a reading, I say yes before I can start thinking about the fear factor. It's usually only later that I start to get nervous.
- Productivity. There is a tried-and-true business principle that a task expands to fill the amount of time you allow for it. If you set aside

two years to complete your book, or six months to paint your mural, chances are you won't get started until the last minute.

Such is the case with my writing student, Vera. She worked full time and was a mom to boot—until last summer when she quit her job. "I used to write at work!" she mentioned the other day. "It didn't have to be good. I knew this was the only chance I'd get so I dashed things out quickly, every day. And they were pretty good, too. But now, I never seem to get around to it because I have all day."

Set deadlines. Hasten to complete them.

Spark

Identify a task and the amount of time you usually take to complete it. This could be vacuuming in ten minutes, balancing your bank account in forty minutes, or answering an email in five. Using any of these techniques, see if you can cut your time in half.

- Play fast music—something upbeat and exciting
- Set a timer and race against it
- Put on sport shoes and run around house or office
- Get rid of any distractions or interruptions
- Fuel up beforehand, with your favorite sports or energy booster
- Race with a partner also doing a similar task for the same span of time

CHAPTER THIRTY

Speak Up

"Speak to me, then, only speak, love."

—from "Speak to Me Mildly," a song by Arthur W. French

IT'S HARD TO SPEAK your mind when you feel your contribution isn't worthwhile. How can you expect others to listen when your whole life you've been ignored? When I began writing a childhood memoir, I recognized how I had learned to stay in the background. I was shuffled from home to home during my early years because of my birth mother's illness. This had left me voiceless. I came to believe that people didn't want to hear what I had to say—unless it was cheerful, short, and to the point.

I loved making up stories for my baby sisters, or writing for school assignments. Yet I kept thinking that what I had to say wasn't important. It didn't matter whether or not I shared. Nobody was going to miss my stories.

After the manuscript was complete, I made a stab at publication, grew frustrated at the market and put it aside.

And then came some telling events (and yes, I'll keep the pun). The next summer, I lost my voice. For several weeks, I had to carry throat spray and lozenges and think on my feet, because I might lose my ability to speak in the middle of a conversation or while leading a class. My voice would come and go, and my throat felt scratched and swollen, and after two doctor visits there was no diagnosis and no improvement. Finally I visited my naturopath.

She gave me medicines and suggestions, but there wasn't a clear picture of what was happening. She continued to ask questions as we sat in her office. After a long pause, she looked at me and said, "One more thing. Could it be that you have silenced your own voice? *What is it that you're not saying?*"

Illnesses can be the body's metaphors for what is wrong in our souls. I'd heard this. But I shook my head. I was teaching and coaching writers. I was doing what I loved. My family was well. I was writing.

And then it came to me: I had filed away that account of my confusing, scary childhood. I had developed my own voice. I had spoken out to the world. And then I had gone quiet. I'd reverted back to my old conditioning: *who cared anyway?*

She repeated, "What is it you're not saying?"

I got back to promoting the stories I'd bravely begun to tell. I aired them, shared them, and submitted them to anthologies and literary journals where they were published. Also, my voice cleared up. A cause was never found, but I got the message.

Since that time, I've read my childhood stories in libraries, podcasts, coffee houses, convention centers and living rooms. They have formed the basis for my autobiographical novel. Although it is sometimes daunting, I've learned *it is the survivor's job to tell the story.*

You've survived, too. You have lived through situations where it seemed you were alone in your experience. Even if you tell your story falteringly, you do have one.

Start small, with the art that comes easy to you. Email a poem. Submit an article you've thought of submitting. Write a letter in your most beautiful prose. Read aloud to the bathroom mirror. Never be ashamed, and never allow that voice to shrink away to silence.

Spark

Write down a bold statement such as "I'm a soon-to-be published novelist," or "I'm a survivor of incredible circumstances." Say something true about who you are and where you're going, which you may never have voiced out loud. Here are ways you can use your statement:

- With an acquaintance you just met
- In a Christmas card
- Making small talk with a stranger
- In a bio describing yourself
- On a blog
- In an article
- On your mirror
- On a T-shirt in fabric marker

CHAPTER THIRTY-ONE

Shut Up

"Silence, silence, make no noise nor stir."

—from "Silence! Silence! A Serenade," a song by J.L. Koethen

I ONCE HEARD AN AUTHOR explain her policy never to talk about what she was working on. Was it because she wanted to protect her ideas? No, she told us. It was because if she began *speaking* about her project, she would lose that energy that whispers at the base of one's skull, at the tips of typing fingers, *Gotta tell someone.* Once she'd told that story, she would lose the need to write it.

Let me say again that we all need to speak up and tell our story. But we also need to be mindful of where we are on the Creative Journey. When you're hanging out at Draft Camp, stay in the wilderness.

When you're at the Playground, don't describe everything you're going to do, just get up on those swings and slide down that slide.

There's a time for speaking and a time for silence: don't let chatter leach away your creative work.

You can find someone to talk to all day long. With a few clicks of the mouse or jabs at the cell phone, you can be texting, emailing, instant messaging —anyone, anytime, anywhere. Likewise, social networking is one of those activities that gives me the illusion that I'm communicating. It takes away my hunger to share with my viewer or reader, who is more or less unknowable.

This is akin to slowing down and handling distractions as in the previous chapter. Again, it's not a popular concept. You don't know what you're missing, though, until you break from the chatter and discover a whole new you, bursting with insight and can-do creativity. Try it, and see if you don't get at least one amazing new idea during your quiet time.

Spark 1

Make a plan to spend time without Internet capability, smart phone, handheld device, or telephone. Don't text or talk to anyone for the entire period. Toward the end of your allotted time, write a letter by hand to a friend or family member.

Spark 2

Do the above for an hour's block of time. Next, try it for three hours. Next, eight hours. Work your way up to 24 hours and beyond.

CHAPTER THIRTY-TWO

Energy

"Energy and persistence conquer all things."

—Benjamin Franklin

I KEEP A WATCH OUT for what energizes and drains me. This is what creative people must do. Each of us is unique, and we'll never learn how to function by following the masses. You must pay attention to your own mind and body.

Mihaly Csikszentmihalyi, psychologist and researcher, writes extensively about "creative types." In an article for *Psychology Today* (1996), Csikszentmihalyi explains that when creativity is needed, some people can "focus it like a laser beam," and when it is not needed, these individuals "immediately recharge their batteries." In what conditions are you most productive? When are you better off resting? Track factors that influence you. Your energy will vary depending on whether you are introvert or an extrovert. It will change depending on physical health, stamina, and amount of sleep. A host of other things can affect you as well.

When I started leasing a writing space three years ago, I was soon using it for meetings only. It was charming but dark, so I tried new décor, lighting, a fountain and harp music. "It's so serene," said an associate. But after an hour max, I was always dying to get out of there.

I had the opportunity to move to a larger space with a huge picture window. Immediately, I began using the office for writing, looking out over the tidy lawns of the uptown neighborhood. Natural light is a tremendous source of energy for me. Without it, I'm restless and drained, especially in the darker months of the year.

On a similar note, your creative space can have a huge impact on your energy, as Feng Shui experts teach. Are you best at home, or do you benefit from getting away? Don't stress if you can't afford an office or studio, but look around for creative options. My own office adventure began when I found an office mate to split the rent.

Also, I've tried various techniques for writing around my family. I can shut a door, mask sounds with mood music, and communicate how much time I need. These things help around my kids, but very few have helped me work around my husband. In fact, just now writing this chapter, my husband burst through the door, having spent Sunday afternoon doing odd jobs for his parents. As soon as I heard his foot-stomping and door-shutting, I knew I'd have to concentrate extra hard. My creative energy is at odds with his chore time, so I'm better off using other spaces or working when he is watching TV.

He's gone outside to work on the gutters, now, and I've lowered the blinds, not to be distracted by the guy on the ladder.

It's interesting, though, how the people we dearly love can drain us of energy. Others, perhaps even casual friends, have a quality which enables us to settle down and accomplish more. These are the people we want to take into account when designing our work flow.

Some times of day jive with my writing, and some don't. Some times of year are more energizing. Writing during the hottest days of the summer, for example, puts me in slow motion. The weeks surrounding Christmas are not great for productivity, but provide lots of opportunities to catch up with other creators through gatherings.

Similarly, online activities drain my creative energy, but can be fruitful in networking. Snacks of raw veggies create energy I can feel almost immediately, but when I dip into the chips or sweets, I'm likely to hit the wall.

Other energizers: yoga, walking, art, and taking an "unscheduled day" to do whatever I want, without a plan.

Spark 1

Find a photograph of yourself feeling at the peak of energy. At a party, on a hike, holding a child. Write the story behind the photograph. Or paint that scene, capturing the energy there.

Spark 2

For one week, carry a paper or handheld daytime calendar with hour by hour increments. Record the highs and lows of your productivity. At the end of the week, review this log and make changes in your schedule to capitalize on your energy flow.

Spark 3

Make a list of ten things that deplete your energy. What can you eliminate, or at least cut down?

Spark 4

What are three things you're doing that help you find more energy? How can you increase these actions and their benefits?

CHAPTER THIRTY-THREE

Torch Your Excuses

"Hesitate, Hesitate, it's a trick that's as old as can be."

—from "Love's Hesitation," a song by Maurice E. Marks

DR. CODGER hates looking silly, being vulnerable, admitting to weakness or fear. That's why he'll often jump in and "help you" by making excuses for not creating. You'll need to dig deeper regarding your true fears and motivations.

One of my Wildfire Writing students, Bambi, is writing a funny and insightful book about weight loss. Today's chapter had to do with all the excuses a person uses for *not* dieting.

Creators, likewise, have many excuses for not creating. Here's an entry from my journal, a little chat with myself.

I have to say that what's keeping me from writing is myself. I've had many excuses (sigh), as to why I don't stretch myself to my writing potential. My latest excuse? My writing coaching business. Giving service to others. It's true, my schedule can challenge me, but I don't really have an excuse. I am avoiding writing because I am avoiding writing. I'm not willing to work that hard.

Being honest takes a lot of courage; it means I take responsibility for how I spend my time. Another excuse is being a mom. "Can't write! I have to drive B somewhere!" Mmmn, no. I can re-

configure things. There are other ways to do things, other means of transportation, and plenty of helpers when I ask.

There's something in me that says my need to write isn't as important as other people's needs. There's a conception that my business is the priority, and that my writing is always lesser. This isn't true though, because my business has sprung from my writing. My own creating has always come first, and must continue to do so.

Now, if I had a writing boss, I would not let regular interruptions happen. The needs of my family would still be met, but at other times, and not always by me. If I had a job that required me to be at my desk at 8:30 am, I would be there, not driving B, not working at my second job, not doing anything else.

See an excuse for what it is. Christi, you have all the opportunities you need. Seize the time that you have. Maybe you're not always comfortable. Maybe you're tired or busy or distracted—but you can do it!

I don't need a different life. I just need to follow through with what I know every day, say no to things, and take hold of opportunities.

This pep talk worked. The following week I clocked in twenty hours of writing.

Now we're going to lighten up and have fun with our excuses.

Spark 1

Draw a picture of yourself in a situation that would *truly* prohibit you from creative work. Perhaps hanging upside down by your ankles from a helicopter over the Sahara desert. Or being surrounded by six hundred natives of the Pygmy Nerd tribe, all wearing poison-tipped helicopter beanies.

Spark 2

Write the most complicated, outrageous, multi-part excuse you can.

Spark 3

Here's an Excuse Maker you can tailor to your own situation, whenever tempted. Circle your choices.

Excuse Maker

I can't write (make a mosaic, finish a novel, enter a photography contest, train for a marathon, sing in a choir, act in a play, paint a picture, write a short story, start a blog, sketch a landscape, craft a poem, write a script, start a journal, practice an instrument, dance, play piano) because my child (family, husband, wife, partner, mother, father, boss, best friend, church, neighbor, pet, job, Achilles heel, sciatica) requires me to spend time with (drive, feed, entertain, accompany, serve, visit, help, focus on, rest, treat) him (her, it) right now (today, for a while, all year, this decade, until our house sells, until after the holidays, until the situation improves, until I make enough money, until they move out, until I retire, until I can't do it anymore).

CHAPTER THIRTY-FOUR

The Fear of Success

"If you don't watch out he'll get you without a doubt."

—from "The Yama Yama Man," a song by O.A. Hauerbach

YEARS AGO I met a writer-illustrator at a book signing. I admired his work and told him I was a beginning writer and aspiring artist. He looked me in the eye and lowered his voice as if tell me a great secret. "Thing is," he said, "most people are afraid to be really good. *Don't be afraid to be really good.*"

Why is it that success can be as frightening as failure? Perhaps even more so.

I've met many talented people who were terrified of using their talents. This doesn't seem to make sense. But taking this fear apart reveals the inadequacy we all feel sometimes.

The fear of success is directly proportional to the stakes we place on it. Paying attention to my deepest misconceptions, I've found this dialogue taking place in my head:

- *I have to succeed . . . or else I'm nobody.*
- *I have to succeed . . . or no one will love me.*
- *I have to succeed . . . or my life isn't worthwhile.*

These consequences are devastating. With that ultimatum, no wonder the idea of success makes me feel conflicted. I'm walking a plank a thousand feet off the ground, rather than balancing on a curb. Even though I might be perfectly capable of doing it, I'm terrified and shaky.

Our first task, therefore, in facing the fear of success, is to tell ourselves the truth about success. Webster's defines success as: *the favorable or prosperous termination of attempts or endeavors.*

In other words, success means we did something that ultimately worked. It means a work of art sold, a book was published, or we got a role in a TV commercial. We worked hard at a skill, improving it, and somebody noticed. Contrary to popular belief, it doesn't give our lives significance or make us worthy to walk this earth.

Make your own personal definition of success. It might be:

- The ability to do work I enjoy
- Rich, fulfilling relationships
- A sense of inner peace
- Enjoyment of this moment
- A feeling my life is "good enough"
- The opportunity to create

The Cal Poly Study Skills Library offers questions about the fear of success:

> *Did significant others in your life often make you feel that way? Were you taught to minimize your success? Why is success so scary? Will it make you stand out in the crowd? Do you feel as though others will not accept you if you are successful?*

Additionally, Cal Poly suggests ways to deal with "self-downing," the fear of success.

- *Practice accepting compliments about your work performance by simply saying "Thank you."*
- *Remember to compliment and praise yourself for work accomplished.*

Spark 1

On an index card, write "Success According to Me." List ten signs of success, internal rather than external. Instead of approval, earnings, and accolades, write about good feelings and personal accomplishments which no one but you need know about.

Spark 2

Notice the "successful" people in society who have problems. Start seeing that the working media definition of success isn't really success. Draw a political type cartoon in which you lampoon a "successful" star.

Spark 3

Fill out the following Success of the Moment Certificate, and wave it around whenever you begin to doubt yourself. Disclaimer: this is a feel-good exercise.

Success of the Moment

Complete this form, circling all that apply.

I,_____(print name), am a

success today, _____ (date), at _____

(time), simply because I am (vertical, awake, out of bed, smiling,

breathing). I am a worthy human being here to experience life, and am

doing so today with every functioning sense that I have. When I look

around, I see_____. What my ears are hearing is:

_____. I am taking in the scent of _____

and the taste of _____. I can feel (the chair under me, the

couch, the sofa, the driver's seat of my car, the carpet, the front porch

steps, the concrete pavement, the wood patio, or _____).

My emotions right now are: _____. I have

lived on this earth for _____ years. No accident, disaster, illness,

heartbreak, catastrophe, war, betrayal, breakup, failure, or disappointment

has been able to destroy me. I am here, a living creative being, a success of

the moment. Hurray for me!

Signed: _____

CHAPTER THIRTY-FIVE

Fear of Failure

To a Toddler Taking First Steps

Don't go so fast!

What if you fail, kid?

You might fall down! What if you crash? Have you thought about that, huh?

Remember last time? You fell.

Remember? You bonked your head.

You're going to fall again! Don't do it! Don't try!

Besides, your legs aren't long enough.

You don't have the experience.

Your friends will laugh at you.

Don't do it! It's too risky!

It could hurt!

Don't you remember what it felt like last time? You cried your head off!

Stop. Just stop it. Right now.

Sit down. Go back in your playpen, carseat, crib, jogging stroller.

Let others take you.

That's it. Let them belt you in.

Why change?

You don't need to go anywhere—you're just fine!

Why move? Why walk? Why try?

It's not necessary. It's not worth it, kid.

Please just forget the whole thing.

CHAPTER THIRTY-SIX

From Boredom to Bonfire

"Behold in me a tired man in the race of life."

—from "I'm Tired," a song by William Jerome

YAWN. HO HUM. *What else ya got?*

Boredom is a sure sign of Dr. Codger. He takes life at face value, not finding anything to pique his interest. By contrast, Dream Kid is curious about everything and can dig into the most mundane event or object with utter fascination. This yields one discovery after another.

Mihaly Csikszentmihalyi has done extensive research about what makes people creatively fulfilled. In *Creativity: Flow and the Psychology of Discovery and Invention,* he explains that people thrive on discovery. Human beings feel most alive whenever they are involved in some kind of discovery, whether cooking a meal or hang gliding or playing a new board game. Discovery is the heartbeat of creativity, while our snap-judging minds crowd it out.

Step beyond Dr. Codger, past the "boring threshold." You can make a new discovery even when you've experienced a thing a hundred times before. This is similar to "The Gaze" in Chapter Fifteen. Focusing your attention moves you to a deeper level. Pushing through the boredom will disable that old critical codger and take you into inspiration. When you know how to access this sense of wonder, life becomes an adventure—even on a plain old ordinary Monday.

Boredom is a symptom of today's adrenaline-addicted society. We're fascinated by doers and shakers. Don't get me wrong. I, too, admire people who do exciting things. I loved following author Marc Acito's chronicle of several years ago, when, from tattoos to zip lines to Quaker meetings, Marc tried something new every day for a single year, and wrote about it with humor and candor. ("Attack of the Theatre Person," www.marcacito.com.)

In comparison, my own writing seemed pale. I didn't have his gift for assembling experiments and adventures. And then I realized the most magical thing I could do was notice the *extraordinary in the ordinary* all around me. Indeed, this is the perfect antidote for boredom.

As Rainier Maria Rilke wrote in *Letters to a Young Poet,* "If your everyday life seems poor, don't blame it; blame yourself; admit to yourself that you are not enough of a poet to call forth its riches; because for the creator there is no poverty and no indifferent place."

I began to see, write, photograph, or draw one ordinary thing every Monday. A lusterless object or activity became enchanting, every time.

I've used this challenge in Wildfire Writing. How boring can you be? What's the most mundane and yawn-producing topic you can think of? If you will focus your attention for ten or fifteen minutes, experiencing a thing with all your senses: sight, sound, taste, smell, touch, you will find an aspect of it that engages you. You'll develop an appreciation for the object or activity, and beyond, an appreciation for your own ability to make discoveries.

Here's Wildfire Writer Jay Morton in his piece on a boring object:

> *It's a stapler. It's not doing anything. It can't do anything without an outside force acting upon it. It's wiggling a bit. The table is unsteady. Humans are writing. Table moves. Stapler moves. The texture is only visible where the light leaves a dull white sheen. Flaws are visible in the plastic. Things that look like cracks. Potential energy. If it fell, which it won't, but could with assistance, it would fall with a certain force. I feel the sudden urge to smack it across the room. It's too small to cause any*

damage. Round blunt corners. Couldn't open it far enough to staple a person's finger. Maybe a baby's. What kind of person would staple a baby's finger? The same kind of person who thinks "Hotel Rwanda" is the funniest movie of all time. It's not moving now that everyone stopped writing. Poor little Boston. What font is that? I think it may actually be Boston.

Spark

Write about, draw, paint, photograph or sculpt any of these things.

- Brown bananas
- Napkins
- Rain bonnets
- Paper Clips
- Bird seed
- Paper bags
- Broken chair
- Dryer lint
- Knuckle hair
- Shaving
- Lost screw
- Fog
- Barn door
- Sliver
- Skipping
- Yawns
- Paper cut
- Buttoning a coat

- Ironing
- Underwear
- Dirty dishes
- Noodles
- Chewing gum
- Piano bench
- Book spine
- Bathing suit
- Drink coaster
- Pinky toe
- Eye of a needle
- Cracker crumb
- Matchbook
- Goosebumps
- Dead batteries
- Bread heel
- Lost sock
- Snoring

CHAPTER THIRTY-SEVEN

Your Right to Be Wrong

"I tell you, if one wants to be active, one must not
be afraid of going wrong, one must not be afraid
of making mistakes now and then."

—Vincent van Gogh in a letter to Theo, October 1884

RANDY PAUSCH, late author of *The Last Lecture,* talked about the impor-
tance of *doing the right things.* This is not the same as doing things right,
he explained. In his Time Management speech at the University of Virginia
(www.cmu.edu/randyslecture), a year and a half after being diagnosed with
terminal pancreatic cancer, he said, "If you do the right things adequately,
that's much more important than doing the wrong things beautifully."

Is writing the right thing for you? Or perhaps it's singing, gardening,
going for a walk, visiting an elderly friend in a care facility. Chances are, if
you're focusing on perfection, you're not doing the thing you need to do.

If it's right, do it. Even if you're doing it wrong.

One of the most freeing things, in fact, is to do things wrong. Just to see
what happens. In the process, we get to places we'd never go. Once I was
blocked in the process of writing a novel. The voice seemed cheesy to me,
stupid. Every word sounded melodramatic and far-fetched. "Okay," I decided.
"I'm going to write that way on purpose: cheesy, stupid, melodramatic, and
far-fetched." I wrote a breakthrough chapter which was funny and slapstick
and got me laughing. I loved it! I was able to finish the book.

Finding the Right Way

Dr. Codger insists there is *always* "the right way" and "the wrong way."

People can go about filling their lives with a hundred trivial actions, doing them all "the right way." There's the right way to clean an oven. The right way to load a dishwasher or mow a lawn. The right way to operate the remote control while watching TV in the right chair on the right channel where the news is always right. These folks never get to their creativity, because there isn't a right way for that.

As a matter of fact, in creating art, there is so much ambiguity that beginners often wish for someone to tell them if they're "doing it right."

We all get the impulse to find one way of doing things and stick to it. For example, one debate I frequently hear is whether a writer should use strong attributions in dialogue—such as "barked," or "murmured," or whether the writer should use the old reliable, "said." It's a matter of preference and style. There is no right way.

An immature creator clings to one way of doing things, never considering the alternatives. I challenge these folks to look at the effects of their choices. For example, a writer can ask herself, "What is the effect I want to have on my reader?" There are myriad tastes and sensibilities.

In seeking *your* way, find artists and authors who do what you want to do and study their work. It doesn't mean you're mimicking: think of the great artists, who followed schools of thought and influence. If you let Dream Kid play, she will lead you to what you like and help you to know the kind of creator you are. Dream Kid will also lead you to other creative minds who spark your own.

Don't bother pursuing things you don't like. As I heard prolific author Jane Yolen once say, "Never write what you are allergic to."

I apply this perspective to reading. It's perfectly legal to start reading a book, even a classic, and not finish. ("Gasp!" says Dr. Codger.) It's also perfectly legal not to read the book in print, but listen in audio format instead.

One thing I do is "read" classics via a visit to the theatre. I recently saw a play retelling *The Iliad*. It was vivid and engaging in comparison to my attempts to wade through all the Greek names of that ancient work.

The beginner looks for a rule to follow. The artist learns that all things are doable and usable; it's how and when you use the rule, and how and when you choose to ignore it.

As Scott Adams, the creator of Dilbert, has said, "Creativity is allowing yourself to make mistakes. Art is knowing which ones to keep." (*The Dilbert Principle*, 1996)

Spark 1

Make a list of the right things you are already doing in your life.

Spark 2

Draw something you have no idea how to draw. Let it come out wrong.

Spark 3

Write a letter to yourself from your Dream Kid. Write it in your "wrong" hand, the non-dominant one. What can you learn from this part of yourself?

Spark 4

Write a story as badly as you can.

Spark 5

Think about all the times you learned "the right way" to do something, only later to discover a new way. Write about one of these experiences.

CHAPTER THIRTY-EIGHT

Ways and Means

"To him that will, wais are not wanting."

—George Herbert, *Outlandish Proverbs,* 1640

IF YOU'RE COMMITTED to your creativity, you'll come up with inventive ways
to keep that commitment. In my case, I needed a way to make time for both
exercise and writing. I started using a voice recorder on my walks.

At first, I felt weirdly self-conscious. It was like sitting in a glass room,
surrounded by an audience. I felt watched by "the voice" . . . even though
it was my own. I pushed through the awkwardness, and created one of my
most useful habits. It's perfect when walking trails or downtown running
errands on foot. (People just assume I'm talking into a cell phone.) I pursue
creative ideas out loud, at a gentle pace, with only myself as audience.

I challenge you to fit creativity into your routine. If you're a writer, this
might mean getting a voice recorder or an app for your smart phone. Don't
worry about making it fancy. You don't need voice recognition software, or
the ability to turn the audio files into text; that's just Dr. Codger trying to
make everything more elaborate and expensive so you can procrastinate.
Most of the time, my writing stays in the recorder.

This voice journaling brings me clarity. It brings me to a wide open vista.
I can see for miles, no longer worried about how I sound, or how I look. My
voice becomes a companion.

When starving for more art in my day, I lay out pens and supplies on my table, desk, work area, or the kitchen counter. Just having them close reminds me to pick them up and use them. By contrast, if I put them neatly away in a box and out of sight, I'll draw or paint less and less.

When my first daughter was born, I opened a dresser drawer, laid plywood on top, and set my computer keyboard upon it. It was just the right height that I could type while nursing my darling always-hungry baby. I sat in an armchair with a pillow to prop up my child, and hammered out magazine articles.

Sometimes you have to stretch the boundaries of comfort in order to find solutions. Could it be the answers are all around us, but we aren't willing to try something new? Some creators I know have done inventive things, but at first the actions didn't seem natural or doable.

You can spend time with your sketchbook while kids play at a beach or park. On a road trip, let someone else take a turn at the wheel while you brainstorm over a project. On a recent car trip, I was able to create collage cards with all my scraps and tools in a box at my feet.

Bring work to the dentist chair, hairdresser appointment or doctor's waiting room. No more frustration waiting for appointments that have lagged in front of yours. Don't be embarrassed. Work on your stuff.

Move, consolidate, or condense your everyday responsibilities to make more room for creating. I like to cook three or four days' worth of meals all at once, so I can use these afternoons in other ways.

Finding time to be creative can be yet one more creative challenge!

Spark 1

Take a hard look at your schedule with the attitude that there is *something* you're overlooking. Do you really need to wash and iron those dress shirts, for instance? Can you take them to the dry cleaner? What would happen if you gave up volunteering for that committee? Approximate how much time you can save, and then use this time for creating.

Spark 2

Schedule time on your calendar to write or do art. Now copy—or make several photocopies—of the appointment reminder below. Tell any concerned parties that you can't help them with other obligations on this day because you have a Very Important Appointment. They don't need to know what it is.

A Very Important Appointment

My creative appointment is at _____

on _____ until _____.

CHAPTER THIRTY-NINE

That's Insanity!

Get up at 3 am to write? You must be out of your mind!
... exactly!

WHENEVER you disable Dr. Codger you will spawn ideas. One way to do this is to get up before he does. Another way is to stay up past his bedtime. Many writers and creators have befriended the early hours of the morning, or the bleary hours of late night, exactly for this purpose.

The trick is to create an experience that doesn't rely on thinking. Here's how it works for me. I set the stage before bedtime, laying out journal, pen, night light. When space was limited in our house, I put a room screen around my writing chair so I could write in our bedroom in the morning without waking my husband. Now I sneak to the guest room.

Before I go to sleep, I close my eyes and imagine the numbers on my clock to say 3 or 4:30, or a designated time. I tell myself to wake up then, with lots of energy. (Don't forget the energy part.) It doesn't always work, but if I spend a few moments with this visualization, it usually does.

Waking up the next morning, I'm ready for Poet's Hour. I roll out of bed into my chair. I grab my journal and nightlight and begin. What comes forth is strange, surrealistic, fascinating. It's dreams, dialogues, poems. I don't think my way into or out of it. Many times I have the faint sense of Dr. Codger waking up and murmuring, "What's this madness?" but I ignore him.

I make it a point not to get up, get dressed, or look at the day's schedule. Sometimes I start by writing down dreams. Even the most nonsensical image can be interesting and vivid.

I'll get insights into relationships and dilemmas. As I look back through the years, I consult my journal and find that I wrote the answers to my problems during Poet's Hour. The ideas continue to give me guidance and wisdom, as life themes recur.

Through Poet's Hour, I've learned how to be with myself, learned what makes me happiest, and how to follow my own instincts. I've learned to let go and not demand perfection.

Keeping with this, I never edit anything during Poet's Hour. Normally a good speller, it's funny how I forget even the most common word spellings during that time. I don't pressure myself about it though. And I don't feel bad when I can't seem to get out of bed at the right time. Some months, reaching for new material and growth, I'll aim for five or six mornings a week. Other months, I might do it twice. In between, I might attempt and fail by oversleeping—no big deal, I tell myself. Like breathing, I reach for the next chance.

I allow myself to go back to bed afterward, if there's time. I write for an hour, an amazing, productive, off-the-wall hour, and then crawl back into bed for another hour of shuteye. No deprivation, no sacrifice, just a wonderful way to outwit Dr. Codger.

Save your writing. When you look at it later, it will be faintly familiar and surprisingly good, even if it's utterly alien and sprouting antennae. You won't remember writing it. It will amaze you with its rarity. "Look what's here!" you'll want to say aloud, "Who wrote this?"

Spark

Mentally prepare yourself to get up at three or four-thirty or five. Set writing materials close by. Pretend you're going fishing, or Black Friday shopping, or catching an early flight. When you wake in the morning, get out of bed, no matter how strange it feels. Don't adjust to the day by getting dressed or grabbing a cup of coffee. Write whatever shows up, whether or not it makes sense.

CHAPTER FORTY

Now You're Smokin'

"I'm not suggesting that you *change* your game,
but rather change the way you play it."

—Robert J. Kriegel, *How to Succeed in Business Without Working So Damn Hard*

SOME OF US grew up with the idea that work didn't count unless it was backbreaking, distasteful, agonizing. If it was easy or pleasant in any way, then it wasn't *work*. Unfortunately, this kind of thinking keeps us from being productive. According to Alan Gregerman, author of *Lessons from the Sandbox*, companies such as Xerox and Compaq are using young children, ages seven and up, to help them innovate. "So why not," proposes Gregerman, "learn from the people who were never 'in a box' to begin with—that's right, from small children?" In his book, he goes on to illuminate the qualities of children, inspiring us to reenact them. Perhaps it is the very playfulness of children that gives them an edge over stodgy-thinking adults.

Certainly Dr. Codger's cohorts have convinced us that work must be work, no fun in it. And yet, the more we hold to this idea, the less we achieve. When we focus on dreary responsibilities, we block our creative, playful side, the instigator of amazing accomplishments.

If you are entrenched in this false work ethic, you'll put creativity at the bottom of your to-do list, because work comes first, always work. And something enjoyable and fulfilling won't seem to count. Yet think about it. Your creative work *is* work, at its most rewarding.

A side effect to this attitude is a lack of joy in the present moment. Another side effect is procrastination (more on that in Chapter 23), which can seriously detract you from reaching goals.

Once you get past this, however, and allow your fun to count as work, there are other hurdles. For, even in the midst of our most creative endeavors, we encounter tedious tasks which are plainly not fun.

If your goals are hindered by heel-dragging, take a look at the task you're avoiding. It doesn't need to be painful. Seek ways to make it smaller and more appealing, so you'll do it more thoroughly and often. Marketing, for example, is work many creative people avoid. I've held marketing parties for myself and other writers who put off making submissions. We chatted while listening to music, munching cookies, printing cover letters and carting manuscripts to the post office. It turned out to be loads of fun.

For many years, I wanted to cook more creative family dinners, but couldn't find the patience. I'd heard about the value of slowing down and cooking meals from scratch. I tried, but my bugaboo was the rote tasks, especially chopping veggies. I hated chopping. My mind was always on the next thing, getting the food into the pot, and onto the plate. I was on deadline to chop and dice and throw. When a food needed minced garlic, I dashed garlic powder instead. When a dish would be amazing with potatoes, I opted for something that didn't need peeling. And so on.

Except for times I got inspired, meals were rushed and uninteresting.

Knowing that fresh, homemade ingredients were important to me, I examined my approach. How could I chop without racing the clock? One day I listened to audiobooks while chopping: this entertainment helped. It was one step on the journey to making the work fun.

Next I tried listening to music. It, too, was helpful. Except when my family would show up and try to talk to me in either of these scenarios.

Finally, one evening, I willed myself to savor the cooking experience itself. I focused on the textures of the vegetables, the staccato chopping sounds, the green-white of the onion tops, every sensory detail. In essence, I pretended to enjoy what I was doing. To my surprise, I did.

My family loved the great meals I started making. But instead of feeling like I was working harder, it seemed to me that I was working *less*.

In this way, I've found that whenever hating a beneficial task, I can "dig into it" rather than hate my way through it. This defeats Dr. Codger, engages the Dream Kid, and unstops the flow of creative ideas.

I've used the technique when doing laundry, filing paperwork, and cleaning house. Here's a poem I wrote in appreciation of doing dishes.

SINKFUL

Plastic dishpan,
square of scrub pad,
muffin tin, mint-green lid, spatula, spoon,
soup pot with leftover squash of butternut.

I roll up my sleeves.
The drain gurgles, catching its breath,
as dribbles of food rinse away,
trickle-swoosh!

Bubbles rise,
crystal halos sparkle,
angel faces press together,
white lace robes bunch:
Doing dishes? Let us rejoice!

(Later, the crowd thins,
soap angels flatten, their
garments long and lazy.
Bereft of dishes,
clear pools open
in quiet sinkwater.
Below in the soaking deep
lie the humbled crumbs.)

When examining productivity, there are things to consider besides attitude. It could be you are a social person, but you've been working in solitude. Can you work in a coffee shop, surrounded by people? Can you buddy up with another creative person? Can you form a group that will meet often and talk about the creative process?

By contrast, maybe you've been forcing yourself into social situations when you need to work alone. Don't feel guilty or inadequate because of the way you are put together. Listen to your body and self, and take action accordingly.

There may be tasks you don't need to do. If it isn't productive, if someone else can do it, if it can be ignored for a long time, then go ahead and defer, delegate or postpone. Be an environmental engineer, getting rid of pressures and calendar items that bog you down.

Delegation may be in order. Few of us can afford secretaries, but virtual secretaries are all the rage because of their affordability. Another thing to do is look for a teenager in family or community who would be willing to do some tasks. One artist employs her preteen to help with proofreading; my daughter screens and sorts my email.

Another way to make "too much work" more attractive is to break a project into tiny steps. Instead of writing "finish novel" on my to do list, I'm learning to put down, "Complete Chapter 10," or "Write 20 pages this month," or better yet, "Write Page 7 today."

At the top of a page, put down something you've been meaning to write. It could be a story, essay, journal entry, memoir, spy novel, an article for your church newsletter, a short romance, a picture book. Now make a list of all the things you need to do to make it happen. The list may include anything from interviewing your grandmother to taking a specialized writing class, to accomplish your goal. Break these steps down further, into substeps.

Write Rutabaga Baking

1) Get library books on root vegetables.

    a) Find lost library card.

    b) Go to library or get online.

    c) Do a library search.

2) Write Chapter One: "The Beauty of the Rutabaga."

    a) Brainstorm ideas for the chapter.

    b) Write outline.

    c) Write rough draft.

    d) Write final draft.

However you choose, make work a game. Some tasks don't need to be done slowly and deliberately. If you can't get into the moment with them, see how fast you can do these things. Set a timer for five minutes and do the dreaded filing, checkbook balancing, studio cleaning, remembering how in the long run it will help you reach your creative goals.

Most of all, think about how and why you do things. What is the best use of your time right now? What will help you achieve what you want out of life? How can you make it more enjoyable? Rearrange your environment, and where you can't rearrange your environment, change your thinking and attitude. Either do what you love, or start loving what you do, and you'll be more productive.

Spark 1

Make a list of work tasks that aren't essential, which you have put ahead of your creative work.

Spark 2

Make a list of tasks you hate or are avoiding which are necessary for reaching your creative goals. (See Chapter Twelve for more on goals.) Next to each task, write a word or two about a creative and interesting element you could add to the experience.

Spark 3

Perform one unpleasant task, fully present in the moment. Breathe deeply. Think about the details of the sensory experience. Pause and write about what you're sensing.

CHAPTER FORTY-ONE

Small Things

boy's first pencil

th'eraser

tasted

yummy

by Harold Johnson

WHEN WE WERE very young, we were told that everything must get bigger: from the kittens and puppies we held to the books we read, to the wheels we rode. We learned to expect expansion.

"Start small," the saying goes, implying one shouldn't stay there. And we have "starter homes" and "kid meals." But what about the things that are better small? What if we began to appreciate smallness in our creative lives? Small things are often overlooked, but like matchsticks, they can be the start of something powerful.

Thinking big can be intimidating. Following the crowd can lead to traffic jams. By contrast, letting things come in small sizes can open possibilities.

I know nothing more freeing than setting out on a journey with a pared-down pack. I include a tiny length of dental floss, a fingertip toothbrush, a stretchy cloth hat the size of a scrap of cloth. Carrying a small pack means a person can move nimbly, squeezing into an airport line or ducking a fallen tree. You can hop stones over creeks because you maintain balance. You can stow your pack on a train rack. A smaller pack is imperative on a long hike, and prevents injury.

Similarly, going through life without heavy burdens feels heroic. You do more than you dreamed; you're light on your feet and unencumbered. This holds true for physical, spiritual, and emotional burdens. The smaller our baggage, the easier we can journey.

Innovators are making huge strides with small things. Jay Shafer, author of *The Small House Book* (Tumbleweed Tiny House, 2009) is a force behind the Tumbleweed Tiny House Company, which helps people create homes from forty to four hundred square feet in size. High quality materials and eye-catching details are attracting droves of customers. Shafer says, "Living in a small house like this really entails knowing what you need to be happy and getting read of everything else."

Smallness can connect you to happiness. For example, I love small rituals. Every day, I light a candle by my journaling chair, and place the extinguished match in a small antique cream pitcher *just so*. The idea of a small waste receptacle was something I saw while traveling in France. Every inn room had a wastebasket no bigger than your palm. The post office kept its wastebasket on the counter. There was no sense of bother over the frequent emptying. Small enables tidy.

My household, currently, is small. My closest friends are small in number, easier to keep track of. My husband and I love small vacations. I like my business small, allowing time for family, life, and long walks. I like the small office building where I rent an office. I love the prayer gathering I attend, with four of us, or three, or two, sitting by candlelight for a small hour. My smallest iPod Shuffle clips to my coat collar. Small things can be carried, tracked and protected more easily. They bring on quiet appreciation. They don't attract attention.

I've begun making small paintings. They are portable. I can carry these tiny things anywhere. It's easier to keep them in perspective, knowing they don't have to become grand or jumbo-sized.

I have been honored to have had my writing appear in small journals, to have read at small gatherings, and to have performed small roles in church or community theatre. I love primroses and appetizers and small towns. Instead of being famous, as I once thought I needed to be, I have found a sphere of influence where I can help and encourage.

When we're willing to "think small" we find what we didn't know existed. Small things can remind you of Dream Kid, and bring creativity into the moment. Here are some small things to do.

- Bring unexpected but gracious humor into a routine email.
- Wear a funny button or pin, or wild pair of socks or shoelaces. When it comes to my youngest stepson, I don't have to look any further than his feet to appreciate his creativity, because he wears sneakers of different colors. (Oh, and his feet *aren't* small.)
- Take a small detour by foot or car. Drive to work a different way. Research shows this is good for the brain.
- Schedule ten minutes on your daytime calendar for doodling.
- Start a very small notebook to keep in your pocket.
- Eat something small and delicious: a kumquat or a truffle.
- Write micro-fiction, usually fifty words or less, while flash fiction is 500 or less. There are many online venues including *Flash Fiction Online* and *The Drabbler* (samsdotpublishing.com/drabbler/main. htm).
- Try the *Six Word Memoir*. (www.smithmag.net/sixwords) I love this by a Wildfire Writer:

Tina's Life

Married, married, married, married. No more.

- Draw a postage-stamp sized picture.
- Buy or make a miniature Zen garden. Rake the sand.
- Break a project down into *tiny* steps. SARK, in *The Bodacious Book of Succulence*, calls this a micro movement.

- Create a small space for creative thinking. Beneath a tree, in a prayer closet, or in the corner of a room. Arrange with care, giving attention to the smallest square inch. Add inviting details: special stones, a bench, pillow, plant, paintbrush, or book of poetry.

- Think of a small accomplishment you have achieved. Write five reasons why it was important and why you should be proud. Post this on your fridge.

- Repeat the above step, thinking of an even smaller accomplishment.

- Make a list of small things you love. On my list: clementine oranges, acorns, sticks of incense, small potted cacti, tea bags, hatched bird shells, moss.

- Draw a cartoon on your grocery list.

- Write a story on the tiniest piece of paper you can. In the story, include the objects on your list of favorite small things.

- Make one small change in your morning routine by sitting at a different place at the table, or using a special bowl or mug.

- Take a small tour around your block. Pretend you are a smallish alien from outer space who has landed in your neighborhood. Make each step count. Use camera and notepad or voice recorder to capture your observations.

- Make a miniature seasonal display, whether a tiny cornucopia, an inch-high Christmas tree, a spring bouquet or a basket of tiny summer fruits.

- Take a small vacation. Really small, half an hour small. Pack one thing. Close your blinds. Imagine you've arrived at your destination. Wear sunglasses and lie in the sun, or read a book on a blanket in your living room, indulging in a favorite drink.

- Make one small change in your Sunday evening, preparing for the week by setting out a creative artifact or tool you want to use: stained glass, sidewalk chalk, an exotic cooking spice.

- Place a windup toy on the desk of a co-worker or spouse.

- Get a tub toy animal for your next bath.

- Put a new picture in your wallet—of you, expressing your creative self.

- Write a haiku. (First line 5 syllables, second line 7 syllables, third line 5 syllables.)

CHAPTER FORTY-TWO

Big Blazes

"Some very queer things I now will reveal,
Of sights that I saw from the big Ferris Wheel."

—from "The Sights I Saw from the Big Ferris Wheel," a song by Harry F. Carson

MODEST GOALS are not stimulating. So says the author of the provocative book, *The 4-Hour Work Week*. Timothy Ferriss points out that it is actually easier to accomplish unrealistic things. "Having an unusually large goal," he writes, "is an adrenaline infusion that provides the endurance to overcome the inevitable trials and tribulations that go along with any goal. Realistic goals, goals restricted to the average ambition level, are uninspiring and will only fuel you through the first or second problem, at which point you throw in the towel."

This may explain how I've accomplished a few unrealistic things in my life. I vacationed in France when I was a penniless single mom. I overcame a childhood of underprivilege to become a creative mentor. I transformed my lifestyle from sedentary desk-sitting to outdoor adventuring. All of these were dreams I could see no way of fulfilling, yet they were so big, I couldn't resist dreaming them.

If your dreams don't thrill you, maybe they're not big enough. Maybe you killed the big dreams because they seemed out of the question. News flash: if you don't dream them, they *will* be out of the question. But if you start by looking at possibility, big dreams can sidle into view. Wouldn't you rather one or two sneaked through the cracks of Dr. Codger's defenses, and came true? Or would you prefer to block all unrealistic expectations?

Perhaps our hang-up with thinking big is that we don't want to be disappointed. Well, as the Man in Black said to Inigo Montoya in the movie, *Princess Bride*, "Get used to disappointment." Disappointment is part of it all, but Dream Kid is tougher than you think. It could be that the next idea you get will instigate change in your life, neighborhood, family, world. If you'll start by allowing the thoughts.

When I was twelve, my new parents had me read, *The Magic of Thinking Big* by David J. Schwartz. I am forever grateful. Without that input, I never would have planted seeds of positive expectation. I would have stayed realistic, within the bounds of Dr. Codger. After all, I was born into a disabled family on welfare. Like so many, I could've chalked up all that "think big" stuff to hokey positive thinking crap. Thank God I didn't shoot down my big thoughts.

Thinking big doesn't mean demanding big. It doesn't mean showing off for the neighbors, or earning attention. It's about removing limits. Have you ever thought of something you'd like to do, only to talk yourself out of it, because the idea was too big?

Separate yourself from the facts. This could be before you go to bed at night, or at a coffee break, or doodling on a sketchpad. You need a space for thinking big, unreasonable thoughts.

Colossal doings start in the mind. Let your finest thoughts run the show in Dream Kid mode. Don't worry: real life will catch up to you soon enough; you won't quit your job tomorrow or move to Fiji. But you need to hold onto big thoughts for a little while, every day. "Without a vision, the people perish," declares the ancient Bible text. And as Thoreau observed, most people "lead lives of quiet desperation." The masses don't foster big thinking, and they are dying inside, a little at a time.

The next time a dream or project seems too big, do the following:

1. Break it down into ten steps. Then take the first of those steps and break into ten further. Remember, big things are made up of small things.

2. Agree with Dr. Codger, but keep dreaming anyway. "Sure, it's impossible. But if I *were* going to own a log home someday, the first thing I'd do is study designs. I would order a subscription to *Log Home Magazine*." (This was me, seven years before we bought our log home.)

3. Think of something big that has happened to you, which you may be overlooking. It may be a special relationship, a close call you survived, or the fact you live in a beautiful part of the country. Notice that big, impossible things really do happen in your life.

4. Repeat #3, with three more big things.

5. Talk to a creator who has accomplished the big thing you're afraid of. This might mean meeting an author at a book signing, getting a backstage pass at a concert, or talking to an artist at a gallery. Notice that this person is an ordinary person, just like you. Sear that into your brain.

Thinking big doesn't mean you need superhuman faith. It just means you don't shoot down your biggest and brightest thoughts. You say, "It could happen," and "It is possible." If you open the doors of "could," and "who knows?" your big thoughts will duck inside and start hanging around.

CHAPTER FORTY-THREE

Sizzle

"Enlarge the place of your tent, stretch your
tent curtains wide, do not hold back; lengthen
your cords, strengthen your stakes."

—Isaiah 54:2 (NIV)

HEY, CREATOR. Congratulations on listening to that little voice that keeps telling you this is the life for you: shaping what may be, using your imagination and talent. Bravo for heeding your wild dreams, listening more intently to yourself than ever before. Now comes the part of widening your boundaries, giving creativity a bigger place in your life. When circumstances, events and people try to tamp it down and shrink it, square your shoulders and say, "Sorry, hon, but I've budgeted to spend that money on my painting class," or "This rejection letter is only one person's opinion." Go to your creative work and do it. No excuses. No fears. Well—yes, plenty of excuses and fears, but we're not letting them run the show.

Move ahead with courage, feeling all the feelings, asking all the questions. You're not running from yourself anymore, but you're aware of all the parts of you, and your heart is spurring you forward.

Have a conversation with Dream Kid. *Hey, kiddo. I've ignored you in the past, I know. But I've learned how important you are. I love how you've jumped in with ideas, insights, feelings and secrets. Thanks for showing up and reminding me how creative I really am. I'm committing to spending more time with you from here on out. You're the best.*

Now that you've given her a place, promise to check in weekly. Daily.

And don't forget to keep a good working relationship with Dr. Codger. *I appreciate how you've pointed out my weaknesses, Dude. Really, I do. I'm going to use your feedback at the next stage of my work. Take a back seat, but it's good having you on board.*

Nothing has to hold you back from your most creative self. You've got so much to give. It all starts with enjoying, creating, living and acknowledging, *in this moment.*

Thank you for touching your torch to the fire and brightening our world.

Selected Bibliography

Bayles, David, and Ted Orland. *Art and Fear*. Eugene, OR: Image Continuum Press, 2001.

Cameron, Julia. *The Artist's Way*. New York, NY: Jeremy P. Tarcher/Putnam, 1992.

Chea, Terence. (November 29, 2010). Living Small Looms Large Amid Real Estate Bust. *Associated Press*. Retrieved from http://www.msnbc.msn.com/id/40414941/ns/business-real_estate/t/living-small-looms-large-amid-real-estate-bust/#. UJ86PYZmqVo

Claxton, Guy. *Hare Brain, Tortoise Mind*. New York, NY: Harper Perennial, 2000.

Csikszentmihalyi, Mihaly. *Creativity: Flow and the Psychology of Discovery and Invention*. New York, NY: Harper Perennial, 1997.

Csikszentmihalyi, Mihaly. July 1, 1996. The Creative Personality. *Psychology Today*. Retrieved from http://www.psychologytoday.com/articles/199607/the-creative-personality.

Dillard, Annie. *Pilgrim at Tinker Creek*. New York, NY: Harper & Row, 1974.

Dillard, Annie. *The Writing Life*. New York, NY: Harper & Row, 1989.

Edwards, Betty. *The New Drawing on the Right Side of the Brain*. New York, NY: Jeremy P. Tarcher/Putnam, 1999.

Ferriss, Timothy. *The 4-Hour Work Week*. New York, NY: Crown, 2007.

Glover, John A., and Cecil R. Reynolds, and Royce R. Ronning. *Handbook of Creativity*. New York, NY: Plenum Press, 1989.

Gregerman, Alan. *Lessons from the Sandbox*. New York, NY: McGraw-Hill, 2000.

Jansson, Tove. *Moominland Midwinter*. Translated by Thomas Warburton. New York, NY: Farrar, Straus and Giroux, 1992.

King, Stephen. *On Writing*. New York, NY: Simon and Schuster, 2002.

Klauser, Henriette Anne. *Writing on Both Sides of the Brain*. San Francisco, CA: Harper & Row Publishers, 1986.

Murphy, John T. *Success without a College Degree.* Seattle, WA: Achievement Dynamics, Inc., 2001.

Procrastination. Study Skills Download Library, Academic Skills Center, California Polytechnic State University, San Luis Obispo. Retrieved from http://www.sas.calpoly.edu/asc/ssl/procrastination.html. Used with permission.

Rilke, Rainer Maria. *Letters to a Young Poet.* Translated by Stephen Mitchell. New York, NY: Random House, 1984.

Sandburg, Carl. *Rootabaga Stories.* New York, NY: Harcourt, Brace and Company, Inc., 1922.

SARK. *The Bodacious Book of Succulence.* New York, NY: Fireside, 1998.

Schwartz, David J. *The Magic of Thinking Big.* New York, NY: Fireside, 1959.

Stanfill, Laura (Ed.). *Brave on the Page.* Portland, OR: Forest Avenue Press, 2012.

Strunk, William Jr. and E.B. White. *The Elements of Style.* New York, NY: Macmillan, 1979.

Tharp, Twyla. *The Creative Habit.* New York, NY: Simon & Schuster Paperbacks, 2006.

Ueland, Brenda. *If You Want to Write.* New York, NY: G.P. Putnam's Sons, 1938.

Acknowledgments

I am grateful to all the writers who have allowed me to quote them. Concerning the song lyrics that begin many of the chapters, I am indebted to the Lester S. Levy Collection of Sheet Music at the Sheridan Libraries of the Johns Hopkins University.

I want to thank the many people who have shaped my writing and teaching. I'm grateful to Robin Jones Gunn for her encouragement and inspiration. I am changed by the hours of dedication and discovery by Joanna Rose and Stevan Allred. I owe much to educator Nancy Fertig and her wise process. Thank you to all my critique cohorts through the years; I'm grateful for each of my fellow writers around the Pinewood Table. I am indebted to Babs Griswold for her skillful editing and proofreading, and to Charity Heller for her advice and editing contributions. To my dear writing students and clients, you have inspired me as much as I have helped you. And, to my darling family, thank you. You are a part of everything I do.

About the Author

Christi Krug is an award-winning writer whose poetry, fiction, essays, and articles have appeared in everything from international magazines to hand-made publications. She has been teaching Wildfire Writing for Clark College in Vancouver, Washington, for over sixteen years. She is an enthusiastic, disarming presenter, conducting workshops for conferences, schools, and libraries as well as independently. Christi works with writers around the globe as a coach and editor, bringing out-of-the-box solutions. To learn more about Christi, or to get inspired by her blog, visit christikrug.com.